IAN RUSH

An autobiography

IAN RUSH

An autobiography
with Ken Gorman

Foreword by
Kenny Dalglish

Ebury Press
London

First published in 1996 by Ebury Press

1 3 5 7 9 10 8 6 4 2

First published in the United Kingdom in 1996 by Ebury Press
an imprint of Random House
20 Vauxhall Bridge Road, London SW1V 2SA

Random House Australia (Pty) Limited,
20 Alfred Street, Milsons Point, Sydney, New South Wales 2061,
Australia

Random House New Zealand Limited, 18 Poland Road,
Glenfield Auckland 10, New Zealand

Random House UK Limited Reg. No. 954009

ISBN 0 09 185183 1

Designed by Jerry Goldie

Printed and bound in Great Britain by Mackays of Chatham plc,
Chatham, Kent

Contents

Dedication

To the memory of those who perished at Heysel and Hillsborough. To Chester Football Club, for launching my career; to Liverpool and their magnificent supporters, for making my years at Anfield so precious. To Juventus for helping me to grow up. To Leeds United, for giving rebirth to my footballing life. And to Tracy, Jonathan and Daniel for the most important support of all.

Acknowledgements

Just as strikers need their service from midfield, so every sportsman needs the unstinting assistance of a journalist to turn the rambling recollections of his life into print. I would like to thank Ken Gorman for his tolerance and patience. I would also like to thank the *Daily Star* for their help in supplying pictures.

Foreword

by Kenny Dalglish

I will never, ever forget the first time I clapped eyes on Ian Rush. I think it was the combination of that eyebrow-pencil moustache and the corduroy drainpipes that made him such an unforgettable sight! If anyone ever walked into the Liverpool dressing room determined to be the whipping boy, the butt of all the jokes and wisecracks, they could not have done a better job than Rushy did on that first meeting with the rest of the players.

And slaughter him we did – we let him have it with both barrels. What it took him a few months to understand, mind you, was that having a laugh and a joke with him was our way of making him feel accepted. Football is a tough, demanding business and it was always our way at Anfield to use off-the-field humour as our source of relief. Taking the mickey, as we did, was our way of welcoming the new boy. It's when new colleagues ignore you, when there is an edge in the dressing room, that you need to feel worried.

Show me a dressing room without laughter and I'll show you a team in trouble. That's not a joke, either. I have known players whose whole careers have suffered after they joined clubs where they were made to feel unwelcome, where they were met by silence. Fortunately that has never been the case at Liverpool. And once Rushy started to open his mouth and speak up for himself, I don't think he closed it again for more than ten minutes for the rest of the time he was at Anfield! It did not take him long, either, to show us that he could play a bit as well.

I remember his first big game for Liverpool, in the League Cup Final replay against West Ham in his very first season with us. He was called up because of injuries, and he responded by playing superbly that night, even though he failed to score. Once he established himself in the team the following season, he just took off. Strangely, he had not scored a lot of goals in the reserve team – but I think Bob Paisley, who was the manager then, had told Rushy to be a bit more selfish. He took that advice with relish, as he took the whole country by storm.

He was phenomenal. If any defence gave him an inch of space, a split-second of time, you could bet it would produce a goal. Luckily, as the goals went in, so his moustache began to thicken a bit and his dress sense gradually improved as well. We couldn't call him Omar (after Omar Sharif) any more, so we nicknamed him Tosh – after John Toshack, another Welsh striker who was a brilliant header of the ball. Rushy's heading ability, or rather the lack of it, was his one major blemish.

He would readily admit that himself. And yet I can recall him scoring quite a lot of goals with his head. I think that's the hallmark of a born goal-scorer – give them the merest hint of a goal and they'll pounce. They don't care what part of their anatomy the ball comes off, as long as it finishes in the back of the net. And Ian was an absolutely deadly finisher, the best striker I ever played with and as good as, if not better than, anyone I've ever seen.

The two of us seemed to strike up an almost uncanny relationship on the field from the start. People used to reckon that we could read each other's minds. I'm not sure about that, but we did hit it off well, and we were on the same wavelength. Strangely enough, it was something we never practised on the training field, just something that came about by pure instinct. We would talk for a few minutes before a game, and I could give Rushy the benefit of my experience by pointing out the strengths and weaknesses of the particular defenders we would be up against. And once the game had started, I would shout a few basic suggestions, such as telling him to go deep or stay on the centre half's shoulder. Nothing more dramatic than that.

I was given the credit for creating a lot of goals for Rushy. They used to say it was my vision that opened up the chances for him to put away. But really, it was his vision, his knowing when to run and where to run, that was the vital ingredient. I would just hit the ball into space, knowing that he would have the pace and the instinct to be moving there. A player of his qualities could turn a hopeful pass into a great one.

It was fascinating to watch his game develop with experience. He was as brave as he was quick, as he showed one night in Romania with two goals that stand out for me. We were playing Dynamo Bucharest in the semi-final of the European Cup in 1984. We had only scraped through 1–0 at Anfield, and the second leg, before 70,000 of the most frenzied supporters I have ever heard, and against a team kicking out at us at every opportunity, was among the toughest ordeals we ever faced. Rushy had been kicked black and blue, but he never lost his enthusiasm or his determination for an instant. And he shut them all up with two brilliant goals to lead us to a 2–1 victory. Those goals were as much a reward for his courage as for his genius. It's an old adage: No Pain, No Gain. Rushy proved the wisdom of those words that night.

By that point he was also becoming far more than just a dynamic goal-scorer. Rushy was our first line of defence when the opposition had the ball, and would terrorize their defenders. If he wasn't kicking the ball off them, he wasn't allowing them any time to settle on the ball and build their own attacks. I could see the look of grim determination on his face as he used his speed to close down virtually their whole back four.

By the time I brought him back from Italy in 1988, he had blossomed into almost the complete player. By then he was making countless chances for others with his unselfish running off the ball, and with the quality and penetration of his own passing ability. I knew it would take the best part of a season before he regained his full fitness and confidence, but I had no hesitation in buying him back for Liverpool. And Rushy has been a magnificent servant for the club since his return, just as he was before he left for that season with Juventus.

He says that, as he's grown older, he has tried to adapt himself to helping young strikers in the same way I helped his development. Well, I take that as a great compliment. I do believe he has the footballing brain now, and the maturity, to perform that role just behind the front man – and that has surely been shown in the remarkable arrival on the scene at Liverpool of Robbie Fowler, who might well go on one day to challenge all those records that Rushy set. Fowler will be the first to admit that he has learned so much from the Master.

But now Ian leaves Anfield again, this time headed for Leeds United and a new chapter in his career. I wish him well – I hope that Leeds finish just behind Blackburn Rovers and Liverpool this coming season! But I know that he is itching to do well for his new club, and is as fired up as he has ever been. If he steers clear of injury – and if he is given the right kind of service – there will surely be more goals and glory ahead for him yet.

Chapter 1

The Leaving of Liverpool

Wednesday, 17 April 1996

My final days at Liverpool are beginning to flash by – it's becoming a headlong rush towards the end of the season. I was involved in my final Mersey derby game against Everton at Goodison Park last night. I hesitate to say I actually played – I came on for the last seven minutes. But I think I helped, even in that short time. We were losing 1–0 when I came on. I got among the defence and Robbie Fowler snatched an equalizer with a couple of minutes left, so at least our supporters will be able to go into work today without facing ridicule.

Derbies are like that. It's incredible how much local passions are inflamed. I was given a real ear-bashing by Everton fans even when I took part in a kick-about before the game. They must hate me. I guess it's a compliment. After all, I've been scoring goals against them for the past fifteen years. They will always remember that. They know I've scored more goals in these derbies than any other player. And I've enjoyed every last one of them. There's no better feeling in the world than getting the goal that wins the game. I hit four in one game against them a few years back – and that ranks among the great moments of my career so far.

Ironically, I was an Everton fan as a schoolboy, just as Robbie Fowler was. But that makes it all the sweeter to score against them – to show them what they missed by not coming in for you. Robbie will be just as ecstatic this morning as I ever was, the mornings after my successes. You feel no mercy or pity for a club, just because you cheered them as a boy. It was frustrating, having to sit on the bench with the other substitutes for the first eighty-three minutes, though. I know the Everton boys were relieved to see me there. I saw Neville Southall and Barry Horne, two of my colleagues in the Welsh squad, at half-time. Everton were ahead then, and deserved to be. They both said the same thing to me: 'You stay there, don't you dare come on in the second half!'

It's strange to think I won't be part of the usual derby match banter any more. And after all my goals against them, it's ironic to think that it was an injury I picked up against Everton at Anfield back in November that really led to the present situation, where I'm leaving Liverpool in less than a month's time. I knew I had a fight on my hands to keep my place in the team when the manager, Roy Evans, brought Stan Collymore from Nottingham Forest last summer. He cost £8.5 million, a record buy for an English club. Now you don't go spending that kind of money to buy someone to keep in the reserve team. I also knew the enormous potential of Fowler, who would be pushing just as hard for a place in the team. But I was ready for the challenge.

I had done well in pre-season training and thought I would be in the team for the first game. Then, when Roy Evans pulled me into his office and told me I would continue to be club captain, I was even more confident. It was Fowler who started off the season on the bench, with Collymore and myself forming the attacking partnership. It stayed that way for a few games before Stan, who was struggling to make an early impression, was injured and Robbie came in to take his place. Although I stayed in the team – and felt I was starting to play really well – I was a bit surprised when Celtic made a bid for me in early November and Liverpool said that I could talk to them.

Maybe, with hindsight, I should have seen then that the club was ready to let me go. As it happened, the move never really got off the ground. It just didn't feel right for me at the time. Within a couple of weeks, though, I would have been happy to have been playing anywhere. There were just about ten minutes to go in the game against Everton last November when I got the ball, and their defender Joe Parkinson hit me with a crunching tackle from the side. It wasn't a very good tackle; he went in from the blind side and caught me bang on the right knee. It was the knee I was standing on – and it just collapsed under me. Parkinson was booked for the tackle, although I don't hold any personal grudge against him. These things happen in football, in all the heat and excitement of derby games in particular.

I guess I can count myself fortunate that over the years I've had very few injuries. I didn't know the full extent of this one at the time. I had some treatment and carried on playing for the last ten minutes. But when I woke up the next morning, the knee had ballooned up. I went to see a specialist, who told me that half the cartilage in the knee had been shattered by the force of the blow. It was so annoying, because I was really starting to hit my best form. I had micro-surgery on the knee, which kept me out of action for six weeks.

Even then I did not think it was the end for me at Liverpool. I still believed I could win back my place in the side. And when I made my come-back for the reserves at Derby and scored the winning goal, I felt I was well on the way back. But Fowler and Collymore had really begun to hit it off as a partnership. It would have been unfair for either to be left out. I felt there was room in the team for the three of us, with Robbie and myself the orthodox strikers and Stan employed in a more roving role. But it's the manager who picks the team. And, in fairness to Roy Evans, Liverpool were playing well. They had a fantastic second half of the season, and they're probably the best team in the country right now.

It has been frustrating for me, though, having to sit on the bench for so long, and then come on for only six or seven minutes at the end. I would obviously like to be playing a bigger part in things. But I came on against Newcastle when we were drawing, and we won. I came on against Everton when we were losing, and we drew. So I feel I played some part in getting those results. I have heard it said that Roy Evans is frightened to play me for longer in case I score – and he comes under pressure for letting me leave the club. But I don't accept that. I love Liverpool and I won't have a bad word said about the club.

But I was also adult enough to realize that my future might now lie away from Anfield. I'd known that for a couple of months. With my contract up in the summer, Liverpool would normally have started talks about a new one by then. But nothing had happened so far.

In the end I went with my accountant and advisor Colin Hall – I've never had an agent – to a meeting with Roy Evans and Peter Robinson, Liverpool's general manager. If I had no future at the club, I told them I would prefer to leave before the transfer deadline late in March. But they asked me if I would remain until the end of the season, because they had nobody else to cover in case Fowler or

Collymore was injured. I agreed, if it would help them out. It was an amicable meeting – the last thing in the world I want is to fall out with the club. My two sons are both Liverpool supporters and I hope they always will be.

But I knew after that meeting that I would be with a different club next season. It was heartening to see the interest that I attracted. Middlesbrough manager Bryan Robson and Sunderland's Peter Reid, both old pals of mine, want to take me up to the North-East; Howard Kendall, a man I got to know and admire in his Everton days, wants me to join him as a player and assistant manager at Sheffield United. All of them would present really exciting challenges. I've also had tentative enquiries from Coventry and a couple of London clubs, while Monaco have checked out whether I'd like to join them in Monte Carlo, and I've even had American clubs wanting me to join them in the new League across the Atlantic.

But, right now, the club I most want to join is Leeds United. If everything works out, that's where I'll be going next August. I've met their manager, Howard Wilkinson, a couple of times to discuss a move – and I've been impressed with him. He's had a difficult season with the team, who were tipped in some quarters as potential League champions when the campaign started. They've had a hit-and-miss time of it, though, reaching the Coca-Cola Cup Final but then seeing the whole season slip away from them.

What I do know, however, is that they have some great players, and they are a much better team than their present position in the League would suggest. In fact, if Wilkinson gets his way with a couple of new signings in the summer, they could be challenging for the Premiership title in the new season. And that is what draws me towards them. They are a big club with enormous potential. That's what I want. I'm not leaving Liverpool just to be put out to grass. I don't want to join a club that can only think about survival.

I want to be in a team aiming to win the League. I've been a winner for most of my years at Anfield and I don't want the habit to stop.

While I know there are some who reckon that, at thirty-four, my best days are long gone, I am bursting with determination to prove them wrong. I was playing as well as I ever have before my injury. And since then I've had what you could call an easy time of it. I haven't been kicked around for the past four months, like most strikers. They are all tired – and all carrying minor injuries, just as we always do by this time of the season. But I feel fresh, super-fit. Whichever club I eventually join, I can promise them that I will get them goals. I feel more determined, in fact, about next season than I've felt at any time since I first joined Liverpool, as a stringy, awkward and painfully shy eighteen-year-old back in 1980.

Even when I left for Italy, in 1987, to join Juventus, I didn't feel like this. I think, looking back, that when I left them, so much of Liverpool remained inside me. They were always at the back of my mind. This time, though, I'm older and more mature. While it will be a sad day when I finally leave, from that day on they will be shut out of my mind. You have to look forward in this life, there's no mileage in dwelling on the past. I've had time to get adjusted to my new challenge. And I'm ready for it. Sometimes you have to take a knock on the chin, to show that you have what it takes to get back up there. That's how I feel. And I know I'll be more determined than anybody else in my new team to beat Liverpool next season. I'll be the happiest man in the world to come back to Anfield and score. It means you've scored against one of the best teams in the country – and where better than Anfield to do it?

I also feel I can leave Liverpool a contented man now – happy that the club has a good future ahead of it. When Roy Evans took over from Graeme Souness a couple of years ago, things were very different. He had to get through a difficult transitional period after the turmoil that the club had been through. Funnily enough, as soon as he became manager he had clubs asking him if I was available. Manchester City were keen to take me, and so, ironically, were Leeds. He was new in the job, and didn't know my feelings, so he called me in and asked me if I wanted to go.

'No way,' I answered him. 'I want to stay.'

'That's exactly what I wanted to hear,' he said.

Had I left then, I could have been accused of deserting a sinking ship. Now I believe I've done all I can to get that ship afloat again. At least nobody can say I'm leaving them in the lurch. And I'm leaving the club on good terms – and in safe hands. I can hold my head up high when I walk around Liverpool. I feel I have contributed, in particular, to helping the Fowler-Collymore partnership to flourish. I've known Robbie since he was just a fourteen-year-old kid, coming in for training. Steve Heighway, our youth team coach, had told me he had this lad who was already something special. I saw it for myself when I got back a day early for pre-season training and watched the youngsters having a game. The first time Robbie got the ball he made space for himself to shoot – that's a knack that only born strikers possess.

In the seven years or so since then he's developed just as I expected. But he's still been only a boy for most of that time, not taking life too seriously. I don't think it used to hurt Robbie enough when Liverpool lost. As long as he was scoring goals, that was all that mattered. We talked quite a lot about the game – about the qualities of defenders he'd be facing, how to judge your running off the ball, things like that. But I knew he had to learn the harsh facts of footballing life before he would become a complete player. Now I feel he has matured and become a much better player for it. He's learned to concentrate right the way through a game now, he works harder, he's become a better team player. Nobody hates losing more than Robbie – the ruthless professionalism of Liverpool Football Club has rubbed off on him! He reminds me of myself at the same age – that tunnel-vision he has when it comes to scoring goals. Provided he keeps that determination and desire, there is no limit to what he can achieve. He can beat all my goal-scoring records for Liverpool – if he wants to badly enough.

Saturday, 27 April 1996

The most emotional day of my life. Not even the thrill of playing in Cup Finals and internationals can quite compare with my feelings right now, a couple of hours after my last appearance at Anfield for Liverpool. Next time I go there I'll be gunning for them. It seems strange to think that players like Neil Ruddock and Mark Wright, who both shook my hand today, will be doing their best to make life miserable for me the next time I see them there. But it was the 40,000 or so supporters who really made the day so unforgettable.

I had three glorious receptions from them, all told. Our manager Roy Evans pulled me aside about twenty minutes before kick-off and asked me if I would like to have the two teams – we were playing Middlesbrough – form a guard of honour to welcome me onto the pitch. I said yes, as long as Middlesbrough were happy about it. After all, it was a Premiership game, not just a testimonial kick-about. I know Boro's manager Bryan Robson pretty well and he was delighted to have his team join in the festivities. So the players were lined up side by side to greet me when I walked out into the sunshine.

My oldest son, Jonathan – he's seven in June – was asked by Carlsberg to be our mascot for the day. That was a nice gesture on their part, and he went out before me, with John Barnes looking after him. He came to join me to have some pictures taken, then I walked out of the centre circle on my own to a welcome that was overwhelming. I've heard the Liverpool fans singing my name many times over the years, but I don't think it was ever as loud as this. This was my second 'farewell' to those fans – remember that I'd left

Liverpool nine years before to join Juventus. I'd played my last home game against Watford then, and they'd given me another uproarious send-off. But it was nothing compared to today's tribute.

Maybe I sensed on that previous occasion that I would come back to play for Liverpool again. I was that much younger, too, which makes a difference. When you're still a kid so many of the great moments just float right over your head. You don't really appreciate them. But as you get older, you learn to truly savour those highlights. They become special memories, times to cherish for ever. My only disappointment was that I was on the substitutes' bench again, having not been chosen to start the game. I would dearly have loved to have been involved from the start, but it's the manager's job, not mine, to pick the team. I sat on the bench until half an hour before the end, when I finally managed to join the action.

The fans had been chanting my name right through the first half. They became even louder in the second half, demanding that I come on. When I eventually did, I was given another ecstatic welcome. I think I tried too hard to mark my finale with a goal. I was running around like a lunatic, trying to cram ninety minutes' effort into thirty. I had one chance, but I tried to hit it too hard, sending it over the crossbar. If I'd been playing from the start I wouldn't have been so anxious, would have been more in tune with the game – and I reckon I would have scored. But we still managed to win 1–0, which was the main thing. And then, at the end, there was not a single soul who left Anfield before I completed a lap of honour round the pitch.

Even the Middlesbrough fans were joining in the tribute, singing my name as loudly as the home crowd. I couldn't help but let my mind drift back over the last sixteen years as I walked slowly round. Great games, great goals, great victories...they all came flooding back. The ghosts of Liverpool's epic European triumphs,

Kenny Dalglish, Graeme Souness, Alan Hansen, that madman called Bruce Grobbelaar in goal...I saw them all in my mind. I just didn't want to leave the pitch. I wanted to savour these moments for ever.

I had decided before the game that, if I did a lap of honour, I would not toss my no. 9 shirt into the crowd, because it could cause a stampede and fans might be hurt. But when I reached the Kop end, I just felt I had to give them something back for their support. So I took off my shirt and threw it to them. There was a bit of a skirmish but thankfully nobody was hurt. And I gather it was a woman who managed to grab it – she must have been a very determined lady!

I pulled the lads' legs when I eventually arrived back in the dressing room, telling them, 'I'm staying now!' But as I finally managed to sit down in a quiet corner I knew this marked the end of sixteen years of my life. There were no tears. It was a moment of some sadness, but mainly of sheer contentment. I know I have done my bit for Liverpool Football Club over those years. If the fans on the Kop won't be chanting my name any longer, I hope they will have their own memories of me to keep them happy.

I met up with my wife Tracy in the players' room, and with my two boys – my younger son Daniel, who is three, was too young to come out on the pitch with me, but he was decked out in Liverpool colours and Tracy told me he'd been shouting, 'That's my daddy wearing no. 9!' As for Jonathan, he was ecstatic because he'd scored a goal against David James – one of his idols – in the warm-up before the game. His other favourite is Robbie Fowler, which just shows where his loyalties lie! I took Jonathan to the training ground a few weeks ago, when he was on holiday from school, and he was thrilled when Robbie joined him in a kick-about on the pitch. Jonathan's happy about me leaving because he reckons he'll be able to have two football kits next season – Liverpool's new one and the colours of whichever team I'm playing for. He was happy, too, when I got the match-ball from the Middlesbrough game for him as a souvenir. After all, I didn't have my shirt to give him!

What colour will I be wearing next season? I still feel right now that I'd like to join Leeds. But the interest is really hotting up. I have been told that Monaco will put in a bid to take me to France as soon as the season is over. A couple of years in Monte Carlo sounds exciting. And Nottingham Forest are also very keen to sign me. Their manager Frank Clark has spoken to my accountant Colin Hall. What I do know is that nothing will happen until after the FA Cup Final against Manchester United. I'm having a couple of weeks' holiday in Portugal from 23 May – and I want my future sorted out by then.

It's proving a momentous season all round for me – apart from not being able to get my place back in the team. A week or so back I was presented with a gold medal by the local tourist board as the Person Who Has Done Most to Promote Merseyside. That was a great honour – especially for someone who's not even a proper Scouser! But, seriously, I gather that Liverpool's former manager Bob Paisley was the only other man involved in football to win the award before me, so I'm pretty chuffed about it.

The biggest personal thrill, though, was being given an MBE by the Queen a few months back. I was first told I was being considered for the New Year's Honours List in a letter I received from 10 Downing Street a week or so before Christmas. It was very strict in pointing out that the whole thing had to be a closely guarded secret until the list was publicly announced. It was terrible – the only other person in the world who knew was Tracy. We couldn't even tell our parents until New Year's Eve.

I went to Buckingham Palace with Tracy and the boys, and some friends of ours, Ian and Sue Hughes. There were about a hundred of us being awarded our medals that day – and about ninety of them wanted my autograph while we were waiting! Dermot Reeve, captain of the Warwickshire cricket team, was also being honoured. I met him a couple of years back at Lilleshall and got on well with him – I sent him a shirt to auction at his testimonial. I have a lot of respect for Reeve, as a greatly underrated cricketer – and one of the greatest captains in the game. He led his team to the treble, turning Warwickshire into the Liverpool of cricket. It made me feel more relaxed, chatting with him.

But the inside of the Palace is so grand that it leaves you almost dumbstruck. The beautiful carvings and the huge paintings of former kings and queens on the walls are really spectacular. We all lined up to file past the Queen, and when it was my turn she did her best to make me feel comfortable, smiling at me and saying, 'You've been playing a long time at Liverpool now...' I told her exactly how long, then she remarked that the season 'was coming to the really interesting stage'. She asked about Liverpool and I told her I thought we would win the FA Cup. I wonder if she took my advice and had a bet? I gather she has been known to have the occasional flutter on the horses!

I won't have a word said against either the Queen or the Royal Family. I believe it would be a sad day for Britain if we did not have a monarch. Our Royal Family is the envy of the world. Even the Americans talk in awe about the English Queen. And if some of her family have had their problems, who are we to judge them? All I know is that receiving this honour would have had nothing like the same significance, had it been some politician giving out the medal, rather than the Queen.

It is a very formal occasion, with two soldiers from the Gurkha Regiment standing guard on either side of the Queen. As I was walking from the Palace into the courtyard, one of them came running after me – asking if he could have his picture taken with me! I never cease to be amazed at how famous Liverpool are, right round the world. Tracy and Sue, along with Jonathan, had been allowed inside to watch the ceremony, but Daniel was too young, so he stayed outside with Ian. But some of the policemen at the Palace were Liverpool supporters, and when they discovered that Daniel was my son they allowed Ian to bring him into the courtyard, which meant that he was able to be in the official photographs.

It was a wonderful day. I still can't believe it happened. Ian Rush, from the back streets of Flint, at the Palace! I was particularly proud for my mother and father. My dad, Francis, is seventy-three and has been suffering from pneumonia. That's what kept him away from Anfield today. Luckily, I've managed to get a video of the game for him to watch, which will cheer him up – he's been supporting Liverpool for some fifty years now and hates having to miss home games.

Sunday, 5 May 1996

The last day of the Premiership season, my last appearance in that famous Liverpool red shirt – and, for Manchester City, their last game as a top division club for at least a year. It's been a funny old day all round, one that sums up all the contrasting emotions of professional football. I was back in the Liverpool team for the full ninety minutes, the first time that has happened since I was injured way back in November. And I had the captain's armband as well – though a lot of folk may have forgotten, I was club skipper before I had my cartilage shattered.

I marked it with a goal, too, my ninth of the season, a blaster from nearly thirty yards, which took a bit of a deflection off a defender but which, I reckon, would have gone in anyway. That put us two goals up inside half an hour, against a team desperately battling to avoid relegation. City showed the courage to lift themselves from the floor and come storming back in the second half to salvage a 2–2 draw. They could even have nicked it in the end. But, at the final whistle, it was despair for their players and the fans who had packed into Maine Road, when the other match results were discovered.

Coventry and Southampton, who had been involved in a dog-fight with City, had also drawn, so it was City who went down on goal difference. I can't help feeling sorry for their players and their fans. City are a big club, a Premiership club in stature. Like Liverpool, Manchester is a genuine footballing city. And the team has some good players. But the harsh fact is that the final League table never lies. Manchester United won the title because they proved themselves the best team over thirty-eight games. Their neighbours were really hanging over the trap door from the first couple of months of the campaign, when they went, I think, for a dozen games without a victory. Life is all uphill after a start like that.

I know one or two of the City lads quite well. Kit Symons is a colleague in the Welsh squad, while I've had a few beers over the years with Keith Curle. But I didn't go up to them to sympathize. I know that some people would, but I also know that if I was in their position, I would rather be left alone. Saying 'bad luck' to a player who's just been relegated sounds a bit trite to me.

Going back to the goal I scored, I think it was almost inevitable, this season, that if I was to score at all it would be something spectacular. If you look back at my goals over the years, the vast majority of them have been from in and around the six-yard box, rounding off sweeping attacking movements. That's what 90 per cent of a striker's job is all about, in my book.

But watching from the substitutes' bench over the past four or five months I have noticed a big difference. The lads have scored very few what I would call bread-and-butter goals. Everyone seems to want to strike the spectacular ones from long range. What perhaps some players forget at times is that a goal still counts the same, whether it's a two-yard tap-in or a blockbuster from thirty-five yards. I think what happened was that a few months back we hit one of those purple patches, when everybody was hitting goals from long range. About four or five players scored them – and very dramatic they were. But there is a danger that you start expecting this to happen every week. Then, when it doesn't, when those pile-drivers go inches over the crossbar rather than just under it, the goals dry up. That's when you should go back to basics, to playing one-twos or looking for a team-mate in a better scoring position. Maybe that's something the lads will have to remember next season.

I was quite happy with my performance, though. With the FA Cup Final against Manchester United coming up in six days' time, I needed the full workout, as did Michael Thomas, who also played his first full game for a while. I knew I would not be in the starting line-up against United. Stan Collymore had been ruled out for today's match through injury, but he was certain to be recovered in time for Wembley. I accepted that situation. Even if I'd scored a hat-trick I would have been out. But at least I showed Leeds United and other clubs who were interested in signing me that the old spark was still burning. And our fans had given me another rousing farewell – I was starting to feel like Frank Sinatra with all these farewell appearances!

I knew it was the last time I would wear that red jersey, because Liverpool lost the toss with United over choice of strip for Wembley. They were going to wear their traditional red shirts, while we would be in blue. We'd also heard, of course, that United had won the Premiership title that same afternoon with their crushing victory at Middlesbrough. So they would be chasing the double. That would make the final extra special. All I was wishing was that I would be on the pitch at Wembley to try to stop them.

Saturday, 11 May 1996

I don't like loser's medals and the one I collected at Wembley today won't exactly have pride of place in my trophy cabinet. The FA Cup Final was a big let-down for me, just as it must have been for the tens of thousands at Wembley and the hundreds of millions who watched it around the world. To be brutally honest, the game was a bore. I sat and watched for all bar the last quarter of an hour or so, barely able to keep my feet still, I was so frustrated with what was going on.

Knowing that I wouldn't be playing, the whole build-up was a bit unreal. You have to summon up your professionalism in situations like that, you have to prepare your concentration as if you were playing. But Collymore had been fit enough to train all week, so I knew that I would be needed only if we were in trouble. It was still a pretty chaotic few days' training before we left Merseyside to travel down to our hotel in St Albans on the Thursday afternoon. There were suddenly thousands of fans thronging our training ground and Anfield, all wanting autographs and pictures taken, and to talk about the game.

We had a short training session on Friday before Roy Evans announced the team. I felt terribly sorry for Neil Ruddock, who was left out to make way for Phil Babb's return. Razor took it like a man. He plainly wasn't happy, but there was no bleating to the press or anything like that. His chance may well yet come, because I am certain that he will stay at Liverpool – he loves it there. As expected, I was a sub, which came as no great surprise to me – but obviously stunned Princess Michael of Kent, who was introduced to the two teams before the kick-off. I had met her several times before at Wembley, and when it was my turn to shake hands, she stopped and said, 'I can't believe you're a substitute. Please tell me it's not true.'

'I'm afraid I am,' I told her, touched that she should be so concerned.

When the game started, our lads seemed to be overawed by the occasion. We hardly had a kick in the opening twenty minutes, as United started like bombs. They could easily have been a couple of goals up in that spell, but for David James, our best player, who made some tremendous saves. James really has come on in leaps and bounds over the past couple of years. I have to admit that I had my doubts when he first joined us – I didn't know if he had the mental steel. But he has certainly proved himself as far as I am concerned. I believe he's England's best goalkeeper right now. And he had to prove it, as he threw himself around his six-yard box to keep United out.

Liverpool gradually settled down a bit as the players began to find a bit of confidence. But it really wasn't very inspiring football. We never really looked like scoring. United seemed to go back into their shells after that exciting start. It was as if the two sides had so much respect for each other that it made them both frightened. With hindsight, it would surely have turned out to be a much more open and entertaining game if United had scored in that opening spell. That would have made us play.

By the time I came on, I had honestly given up on the chances of either side scoring before extra time. It just seemed like one of those games – Fowler and Collymore, who came off to make way for me, had barely had a chance between them. Then, a minute before the end, it all went horribly wrong for us. James, who had performed so well, collided with Mark Wright as he came out to deal with a cross. He could only palm the ball, which caught my shoulder – I was back helping the defence – as it went out to Eric Cantona. He smashed it home – a fairytale end to the season for him and for Manchester United, but the low point of a dismal afternoon for Liverpool. There was no way back for us, with so little time remaining.

I was angry at the end when referee Dermot Gallagher blew the whistle right on the ninety minutes, with barely a second of extra time played. My frustration got the better of me, as I had a bit of a go at him as we walked back to the dressing rooms. I guess I got a bit heated – at one point he threatened to send me off, even though the game was long over. I don't think he refereed the game badly, or anything like that, but there were at least a couple of minutes of extra time to be played.

Anyway, my final season at Liverpool had ended on a note of acute disappointment, without a trophy. Yet, in some ways, it made the parting that little bit easier. I still felt pretty low back in our hotel after the game. I had a few beers – my wife Tracy had joined me by then – but I was in no mood to enjoy myself. I seemed to be taking defeat worse than some of the younger lads around me. Maybe it's a throwback to the Liverpool side I first joined back in the Eighties – men like Kenny Dalglish, Graeme Souness and Alan Hansen hated defeat so much they could barely tolerate it. And that kind of attitude rubs off on those around them.

There was one consolation, though – I got the 'present' my son Jonathan wanted most of all...Ryan Giggs' Manchester United shirt! It was the last message I had got from Jonathan before I left home for London. While we were in the tunnel waiting to come out, I asked Ryan if he would swap shirts with me at the end. He thought I was kidding him! 'You're just winding me up!' he said. I've known him for a few years now, since he was little more than a boy, when he first broke into the Welsh squad, so he thought I was pulling his leg.

I was quite touched to read a story in one of the newspapers, in which Ryan had talked about me as one of his idols when he was still a schoolboy. I remember doing my best to make him feel at home when he was a rookie with the Welsh team, the way I've always tried to help the younger players to relax and feel a part of the set-up. And I've watched his career develop to the stage where, right now, he has blossomed into one of the most exciting players in the world. He's had to suffer the inevitable comparisons with George Best, which is very unfair on him. You can only be judged by your own peers in your own time. All I know is that I'm delighted he's Welsh – and that he plumped to play for Wales when there were efforts to turn him into an 'Englishman'.

Giggsy was one of the few players who was able to walk off Wembley today feeling he had played well. He threatened danger every time he got the ball, with that explosive pace and beautifully balanced running. He has all the qualities needed to become one of football's true greats – just like my successor at Liverpool, Robbie Fowler.

Somebody asked me whether I would recommend a spell in Italy for the two of them, to further their footballing education. It's a difficult question to answer. When I went, back in 1987, there was an obvious gulf, both in quality and in financial reward, between playing in Italy and playing in England. I feel that playing for Juventus, even though it was only for a year, helped me to grow up, to become a more rounded person. And the money helped as well! But nowadays the wages paid to the top players in the Premiership compare pretty favourably with any other country in the world – Italy included. And I also believe that, although our clubs haven't been very successful in Europe in the past few years, the standard of our top division is getting better every season.

I am certain that the wealthiest Italian clubs will be looking enviously at the two of them and that offers will come in. I would not advise them one way or the other – except to warn them to take a thorough look at the situation before making their minds up.

My mind right now is on places a bit closer to home than Milan or Turin – across the Pennines from Liverpool to Leeds is the next big journey for me. The next time I kick a football it will be in the white shirt of the Elland Road side. I've made my mind up for certain now, that's where I want to go. It was a tough choice in some ways, because I would have enjoyed working as number two – and playing as well – to Howard Kendall at Sheffield United. I've known and admired Howard for years, since he took Everton to the top some ten years ago. The only problem is that joining him would have meant moving down to the First Division – and at my age, I don't have time to wait around, even if they get promoted next season.

I also had a great offer from another distinguished old Evertonian, Peter Reid, to join him at Sunderland, who have just won promotion to the Premiership. That was tempting – I love the supporters up in the North-East. But I still want to be a winner, as much as I ever did in my life. And I believe that Leeds United offer me the best opportunity to achieve that. I've been across to Elland Road to have a chat with the manager Howard Wilkinson – and I'm certain he's a man I could play for. It's fascinating listening to him talking about football in a way I've never really heard before at Liverpool. He's got a reputation as one of the game's deep thinkers, and that's obviously well earned.

At Liverpool, though you would never argue against the footballing knowledge of people like Bob Paisley, Joe Fagan, Kenny Dalglish, Graeme Souness and Roy Evans, they never went in for tactical discussions. I think the Anfield philosophy was to get the best players in the team and then let them get on with it. Enjoyment was also a vital ingredient – even on the training pitch we would always have fun while we worked. A happy, contented bunch of players is generally a successful one – that was the attitude. And when you look at the trophies Liverpool have collected over the decades, it's hard to argue against this.

But I do feel that tactical appreciation is something I need to work on if I am eventually to make it as a manager, which is now very much in my thoughts for the future. I plan to learn as much as

I can from Wilkinson – maybe we can learn a bit from each other. What I also have to do is settle down with Leeds as quickly as I can – in days rather than months. I just don't have the time to spare on such things at this stage in my career. I'm not one of those who keeps the dressing room shaking with laughter every day – there are mornings when I'm feeling so miserable that I don't say a word. But you won't catch me sitting in a corner, as I did when I joined Liverpool.

I just intend to be myself. I have a lot of respect for the other players in the Leeds squad – Gary Kelly and Tony Dorigo are the best full-back pairing in the Premiership in my book, while Carlton Palmer is a very underrated grafter, and Tony Yeboah scored some amazing goals last season. I've also been a good pal of Gary Speed for quite a while – we've played a lot together in the Welsh team – but it seems that he will be leaving Elland Road to give Wilkinson the cash he needs to make two or three more signings. All in all, it looks as if it's going to be an interesting summer at the club, with a new goalkeeper and at least one new defender likely to follow me there.

Monday, 20 May 1996

It's Ian Rush of Leeds United – official! I've signed the two-year contract that binds me to the club until the summer of 1998, although I don't actually join them until 1 July, the day after my contract runs out at Liverpool. I feel relieved now that all the speculation in the newspapers is over. And having spent much of the day with Howard Wilkinson, I'm more convinced than ever that I have made the right move. He seems as determined to be a winner next season as I am. He's got plans to strengthen what is already a powerful squad – and a place in Europe is my ambition. That means winning trophies, or at least finishing in the top four or five in the League. And while that is the target, I believe that if

Wilkinson gets his men, and we gain the confidence of a good start to the season, we could be challenging for the League title.

I drove across the Pennines from Liverpool with my accountant Colin Hall, who has helped to iron out the small print of the deal. One clause I did insist on was an opportunity for me to review my own situation if Wilkinson were to leave. Because Leeds have not done anything like as well as people expected this past season, there has been some speculation about their manager's future. That's inevitable. But it's totally without foundation, I have been assured by Bill Fotherby, the acting chairman. A new man will be taking over at Elland Road in the next few weeks, but I've been told that Wilkinson's position will not even be discussed. He's as safe as houses.

I had to undertake two medicals, at different hospitals, before the signing could go ahead. Naturally they wanted to make sure there were no problems with their investment. But I passed both of them, as I knew I would. I feel fitter at the end of the season right now than I have done for years. Spending so much time on the bench means that I haven't been kicked all over the place, the way most strikers have. The manager also took me to see United's training ground, which looks every bit as well equipped as Liverpool's.

I'm very impressed – so far at least! – with everything I've seen about Leeds. And I got the feeling of being with another big club at the press conference, in mid-afternoon. The place was packed, which I found a big boost as well – obviously I'm still fairly big news in Yorkshire! I had to do a lot of television and radio inter- views, as well as the main press conference, then pose with Wilkinson for a huge crowd of photographers. The one thing I couldn't do was wear a Leeds United shirt. Apparently they are in the process of changing their sponsors to Puma, who didn't want me to be seen wearing the old shirt. Such are the problems of modern football! But someone found a Leeds scarf, so I held that above my head for the pictures.

It was five o'clock before I was finally able to leave for the journey home, which took about an hour and a half – that's a journey along the M62 that I'm going to have to get used to. But it really isn't that bad, as it's motorway virtually the whole way. And I had plenty to think about as I drove home – like the pre-season training, which begins on 8 July. From what Wilkinson told me, it's going to be much tougher than anything I've ever been used to at Liverpool. All the players will have a fitness test on the first day back, when he expects us to be able to complete a two-mile run inside twelve minutes. That might not sound too difficult for Steve Cram, but it's a pretty formidable order for footballers who have spent the summer sitting on beaches and having the occasional lager, or several, to keep them cool!

Wilkinson told me that he gave all the players an exercise programme for the summer – and even gave them a chart to enable them to monitor their progress. He handed one to me as well. But I don't need it, because I am already determined that I will have a pretty good basic standard of fitness by the time I report back. I'm off to Portugal in three days' time with Tracy and the two boys for a fortnight's break – and I'm hugely looking forward to it after all the strain of the past few months.

Right now, my ambition is to get a place by the poolside and stay there! But I know that after a couple of days I'll get itchy feet – and I'll have a few runs round the Algarve to keep me fit. I'm one of those lucky guys who never puts on an ounce of weight, no matter how much I eat and drink. But I don't just want to be slim when I go back to Leeds – I want to be fit. Pre-season training is the most important part of the whole campaign in many ways. If you don't get your body fit then, you'll never catch up.

I'm looking forward to meeting up again in the new season

with Leeds' number-one fan – John Charles, the greatest legend in Welsh footballing history. He still lives in Yorkshire and never misses a home game. I did play for Leeds once before, during my season in Italy, when I flew back to take part in a testimonial game that the club had arranged for Big John. We beat Everton 3–2 – and I scored a hat-trick! It's funny that I've followed the Charles trail to Leeds and to Juventus, where he also remains an idol to this very day. He's never had a bad word to say about Leeds, just like another of their old boys, Terry Yorath, who was Welsh manager for a few years. When former players have only praise for their old club, it means there must be something right about it – and that's a great comfort to me right now. All I really want now is for next season's action to start – and to get my first goal. That will be a great relief...

Chapter 2

Living for Kicks

I t was back in March 1980 that Liverpool first wanted to sign me. And I turned them down! I wasn't being clever or awkward. I simply felt that I was nowhere near good enough to play for them. I was just eighteen years old and had only established myself in Chester's Third Division team that season. There had been a good deal of speculation in the newspapers linking me with Liverpool and Manchester City, two of the most powerful teams in the country. But, quite honestly, I didn't take a great deal of notice. I had no great ambitions. I wasn't really in their league.

Playing for Chester and earning up to eighty quid a week with bonuses was the heady heights for a kid who had to start his career in hand-me-down boots. Life was tough in the three-bedroomed council house in Woodfield Avenue, Flint, where I was raised, the last but one of ten children in the Rush household. My father Francis was a steelworker, working at the nearby Shotton Steelworks until it was closed down. He worked all the hours he could to make sure there was always food on the table. But life must have been a gruelling struggle for him and my mother Doris, who seemed to spend her whole day cooking, cleaning, washing and ironing.

I had to share a bedroom with my five brothers, which made it difficult enough when we were all at school but downright impossible when the older brothers started working. One would be on a morning shift, which meant he would be getting up at five o'clock – and waking us all up. Then another would come home from night shift maybe an hour later – and wake us all up again! It was chaos. To this day I don't know how I got by on so little sleep. My parents went without an awful lot themselves to make sure that we had all the necessities of life. But there was no money for any luxuries. I remember the first pair of boots I ever owned. I got them when I was six years old – and they were probably older than I was! Two or three of my brothers had worn them before me.

Still, I had a lot to be thankful for in those days...like being alive. I was only five when I was struck down with meningitis, a killer illness that has claimed so many young lives. I was in a coma and in an oxygen tent for two weeks at the Cottage Hospital in Flint, where only the dedication and skill of the doctors and nursing staff enabled me to pull through. Even then, they feared I might suffer permanent brain damage. Maybe that's why I was never much good at lessons at school! But, ironically, that illness – I was in hospital for more than a month and unable to eat for much of that time – helped to mould my career. Until then I had been short and chubby, but I lost a great deal of weight, which I never put back on.

That illness is no more than a blur in my memory. But what I can remember, from the days when I was only a toddler, barely old enough to walk, was that football was the family obsession. I was always kicking a ball around the garden with my brothers – most of whom went on to be pretty good footballers in their own right. Then I graduated to twenty-a-side matches on the field near our house. And I was still only seven years old when I was first picked to play for the school, St Mary's Roman Catholic Primary School in

Flint (my parents are both devout Catholics, and I still go to church every Sunday I can).

I scored two goals in a five-aside tournament – and then I was dropped for being too young! Most of the other kids were three years older than me and the teachers felt it wasn't fair to leave any of them out for me. I had three years left to get my chance. It was two years before I was called up again. I was still a year younger than the rest, but the school won the Deeside Primary League and reached the final of the North Wales Junior Shield. I had trials with Deeside Schools, although I didn't win a place in their side that season.

It was the following season, my last in primary school, that I really started scoring goals. I won a regular place in the Deeside Schools side that year and scored seventy-two goals in thirty-three games – a record only just beaten. We became the first side from North Wales to win the Welsh Yeoman's Shield, beating Newport 3–1 away and 7–1 at home in the final – and I scored three goals in the two games. But my personal highlight came in the two games I played for my school against our bitter local rivals, Gwynedd School, which was situated just half a mile down the road. We hadn't beaten them for four or five years. But this time we hammered them 8–4 at their school – and I scored the eight. Then we won 6–4 in the return match...and I scored the six!

John Toshack, the goal-scoring idol of Liverpool and Wales at the time, came to present the Deeside Schools players with their medals at the end of the season. It was a great thrill meeting somebody famous for the first time in my life. All the lads were awe-struck. But although my father was a big Liverpool fan, my team then was Everton. When I got a bit older I used to go to Goodison Park to watch them. And my personal favourite, the only player I really idolized as a boy, was their centre forward Bob Latchford. I vividly recall watching from the terraces, the season he scored thirty First Division goals – not even in my wildest dreams could I see a day coming a decade or so later when I would equal that achievement.

I had my first taste of captaincy in my second year at St Richard Gwyn High School. In fact I skippered the school team, the Flintshire side and the Deeside team. I was still scoring plenty of goals – even though I was playing mainly in midfield! My father used to watch as many games as he could, and he was approached on the touchline during one game by a scout from Liverpool, who took my name and address and promised my father he would be in touch. But we never heard from him again. I was only thirteen then and didn't give the matter too much thought. But it's strange to think that if they had signed me then on schoolboy forms, they could have save the £350,000 it cost them to sign me five years later.

I played rugby union and hockey for the school as well at that time. But it still wasn't enough to keep me out of trouble. I guess teenagers have a lot of energy to use up. And there wasn't much to keep young minds entertained in a small town like Flint. I was drinking in the local pubs from the time I was fourteen. I used to stay off school to go swimming, or just roam the local countryside. Our gang, which was eight or nine strong, was always fighting with other gangs. I even had to spend nine hours in a cell in Rhyl Police Station after a bunch of us were caught stealing badges and packs of playing cards from a souvenir shop.

To this day I am ashamed of that incident. We weren't stealing for personal gain, just for laughs. It was absolutely stupid. A policeman caught us as we ran out of the shop and hauled us down to the local nick, where we had to stay locked up until our parents eventually arrived to take us home at two o'clock the following morning. I was still only fourteen and scared stiff, and disgusted with myself for letting my parents down. They had sacrificed a lot on behalf of their children – and here I was behaving like some tearaway. I had to go to court, which was another frightening experience. I feared I would be locked away. But while some of the other lads were fined, I was given a conditional discharge for two years because I was younger than them.

The whole affair taught me a lesson I never forgot. I think it knocked a bit of sense into me. I started to realize that life was far more than just a few cheap belly-laughs. Before my fifteenth birthday I had signed schoolboy forms with Chester, which kept me busy training with them after school. I also enjoyed my first taste of international football, playing for the Welsh Schools Under-15 team against Scotland in Perth. We won 1–0 – and I scored the only goal, nipping in to latch on to a faulty backpass and side-footing it past their goalkeeper. It wasn't a classic, but it was a goal, a memory I will always cherish.

I went on tour with the Welsh team to West Germany and France, where I had my first real taste of big-time football. We played France at the famous Park des Princes Stadium in Paris, as the warm-up to a full international. So there were about 20,000 watching us at the start – and a lot more by the end. It was a nerve-racking experience for all of us, who had been used to playing before no more than a few hundred people, maybe a couple of thousand at cup finals. But we played quite well, to force a 1–1 draw.

I spent that summer of 1977 gaining my first experience of professional football – helping to paint the rickety old grandstand at Chester's Sealand Road ground. I also had to clean out the dressing rooms and generally get the place ship-shape for the coming season. This was my idea of a dream come true, being allowed to wander round a proper football stadium. It stopped me getting into mischief – and they even paid me five pounds a day expenses. I also had a newspaper round in the evenings, so I was a wealthy man!

I had one more year left at school. And it turned out to be the most frantic time of my whole life, footballing-wise. Apart from playing for the school team most Saturdays, I played local football for Hawarden Rangers on Sunday mornings, played for Chester's youth team, the Welsh Under-18 Schools team – and the Great Britain Catholic Schools Under-18 side for good measure. Three games a week constituted a quiet spell – I was often playing four or five times a week. My most abiding memory came while playing for the Catholic Schools' team in the annual European competition, which was held in England that year. We played Italy in one game – and they had three players sent off. They were just kicking lumps out of us. Talk about religious fervour! But we kept our heads and hammered them 13–2 – of which I scored five. The season had a down-side as well, though. Chester's youth team lost 9–1 in the FA Youth Cup to Oldham, still the heaviest defeat I've ever suffered.

Back at school, most of my teachers and the careers officers who used to visit us thought I was bordering on the insane when I told them I wanted to be a footballer when I left. They wanted me to take up an apprenticeship as a car mechanic, a bricklayer, jobs like that. I've nothing against such jobs – they're far more important than football, when you think about it. And, looking back, I can understand their concern for me. After all, for every boy lucky enough to make it in the harsh world of professional football, hundreds fall by the wayside. They wanted me to have a career to fall back on if the football didn't work out. The trouble was that at sixteen you've got stars in your eyes. Caution and common sense are way back on the agenda.

Cliff Sear, the youth team manager at Chester, had already promised that the club was going to take me on as an apprentice for the 1978–9 season. Nothing else mattered. I didn't do too badly in the end of school examinations – I got five CSEs, in English, Mathematics, Humanities, Geography and Art. I joined Chester that summer – but it could easily have been Manchester United. A scout from United had watched me playing in my last year at school and had contacted my father, asking if we would like to go to Old Trafford for lunch and meet the players. He even asked me when I had my next holiday from school, so that he could arrange the visit. I was thrilled and so was my father. But we waited and waited – and heard nothing.

Then, after I had already agreed to join Chester, he came back and told me that United would take me onto their staff as an apprentice. I had not actually signed for Chester, so I could have reneged on my agreement with them and gone to the much more glamorous surrounds of Old Trafford. But my father would have none of it. 'You've given your word to Chester, now you have to honour it,' he told me. And he gave the scout pretty short shrift!

He was right, of course. You have to have some kind of moral code in this life. That's why he hit the roof when a big Midlands club tried to sign me – and offered him a lot of money if he could persuade me to join them. Such an offer was totally illegal under Football Association rules. And he told the club concerned, in no uncertain terms, where to go! He certainly wasn't a wealthy man, and the money would have been more than useful. But his principles were far more important to him than the cash. I have to admire him for that.

As things turned out, joining small-time Chester helped my career take off in a way that it might never have done at Manchester United or with that Midlands club. Quite a few clubs had made overtures towards me while I was still at school, and I went for trials with three of them – Wrexham, Chester and Burnley – before plumping for Chester. Burnley was the club with the biggest reputation for churning out youthful talent, but I found the set-up there a little bit overpowering. It was well organized but almost regimented. I didn't think there would be any time for a smile and a joke. Wrexham were the opposite. Their training was a shambles, about thirty or forty players all just milling around on a Sunday morning. But Chester seemed just right. There were only three other schoolboys training there with me, so we used to join the first-team players, which was a great thrill for us – and a quick way to learn the tricks of the trade of the professional game.

I had already gained a pretty good insight into the club by the time I left school to join them as a sixteen-pounds-a-week apprentice. For the first month or so I saw more of a paintbrush than a football, as I had to help to spruce up the ground again. But it was my first taste of pre-season training, after all the players reported back, that produced the first real eye-opener into the life of a professional footballer – and a murderous one it was.

Having been playing football and running into and away from trouble for most of my adolescent life, I thought I was a pretty tough, fit sixteen-year-old. I was fooling myself! That first day of training began with a gruelling four-mile run, followed by a lung-bursting sprint session, then half an hour's weight training. After lunch we had a full-scale practice match, then more sprints to round the day off. Then, when the senior pros had left for home, we apprentices had to clean up the dressing rooms in readiness for the next day. I staggered home to tea and then collapsed, exhausted, into bed by eight o'clock in the evening. So much for the glamorous world I was just entering. It didn't get any easier, either. We endured the same shattering routine day after day.

The bit I hated most was the distance-running. I was a fair sprinter, but I must have lacked the strength and stamina for the longer stretches. A four-mile run was purgatory for me. I used to end up anything up to half a mile behind the rest by the finish. Alan Oakes, the team's player-manager, even began to give me half a mile start – and still I'd trail in behind the rest. Then Oakes and the players would hand out some real verbal punishment. I felt humiliated, and thought he was being tough in the extreme on a young lad like myself. What he was doing, of course, was geeing me up. And in the end it worked. I would grit my teeth and be grimly determined not to be laughed at the next time. By the end of pre-season training I could at least keep up with the pack. I was never going to be another Brendan Foster, but at least I was the object of derision no longer.

I spent that first season in the reserve and youth teams under the guidance of Cliff Sear, who helped to mould my career as much as anybody. Our reserve side played in the Lancashire League, where most of the teams possessed a smattering of hardened old pros. That experience also toughened me up. They didn't take kindly to the idea of some young kid making them look foolish – so they would stop me any way they could. I learned the hard way about the crafty knocks behind the referee's back, the obstructions, the 'mistimed' tackles that could maim you if you were not careful.

This was football the way the professionals played it – light years away from the game I had played at school and in the local leagues. It was a fascinating – if sobering – lesson. I was always fortunate, even in those far-off days, in being able to keep my temper under control on the field. I always felt that the best form of retaliation was to score a goal. So even when men twice my age were trying to kick lumps out of me, I would content myself with giving them a withering look and getting on with the game. Ironically, I was booked once that season, for nothing more sinister than a mistimed tackle. But it was significant, because I was not to have a yellow card flashed in front of me for another five years, when I was playing for Wales against Bulgaria at Wrexham in April 1983.

I scored a few goals that season, but nothing to get excited about. It didn't, however, stop Cliff Sear from building up my reputation in the local newspapers. He told them I was the best prospect for my age that the club had possessed in years. If that made a few supporters sit up and take notice, it cut no ice among the senior players. Part of my job was to clean the boots of the first-team centre half Bob Delgado, probably the chirpiest character at the club. He was certainly the strongest. He would pick me up and sling me into the bath if there was the slightest speck of dirt on his boots. As you might guess, I had more unwanted baths than I care to remember!

I had my first wage rise on my seventeenth birthday – up from sixteen pounds a week to twenty! It meant I could pay eight pounds to my parents and still have enough left over for a booze-up every Saturday night. But the season passed uneventfully until the very last game, when we were at home to Sheffield Wednesday. I arrived at the ground at two o'clock to lay out the team kit, when Alan Oakes called me into his office and told me that I was playing – in midfield. 'Just do the simple things, don't try anything special,' he told me. I didn't have time to feel nervous, I was out on the pitch before I knew it. I didn't do an awful lot, but we drew 2–2 – and I was content just to have sampled the experience of first-team football.

I was officially called up because Oakes had ruled himself out through injury. But, with hindsight, I am certain that it was a deliberate ploy by Alan, to take away from me that element of fear of the unknown. We were in mid-table, it was our last game of the campaign, with nothing at stake...a perfect chance to blood a young player.

I was on the fringe of the team by the start of the new season, 1979–80, notching my first senior goal at Gillingham – a right-footer from all of eight yards out. It came five minutes from the end, to give us a 2–2 draw. And if it wasn't the most spectacular goal I ever scored, I still get a kick just talking about it. It's one of my most cherished memories.

My first real break came a month or so later, however, when our centre forward and top scorer Ian Edwards was sold to our local rivals Wrexham for £125,000. The transfer created a furore among our supporters, who thought Oakes was insane to let the club's top asset go. There were a couple of young players I thought were ahead of me in the queue to take Edwards' place, but a few days before our next game I was tidying the treatment room while Oakes was receiving attention for an injury.

He was chatting generally about what a great loss Edwards' departure would be when he suddenly looked up at me and said, 'Son, I think you're the player to take his place.' I didn't answer at first. I was too stunned. He asked me, 'Well, are you up to the job?'

All I could muster in reply was a feeble 'I dunno.'

So he asked me again, 'Do you think you can do it?'

I took a deep breath and told him, 'I'll give it a go.' That, thankfully, was enough of an answer for him. I was given the no. 9 shirt the following Saturday and kept it for the rest of the season, scoring seventeen goals in thirty-four games.

We were only a Third Division team but we had a wonderful run in the FA Cup that season, reaching the fifth round – the furthest the club had ever got. I notched up my first Cup goal at Workington in the first round – I scored two, in fact, as we won 5–0. But the highlight was our third-round tie, away to Newcastle United, who were romping away with the Second Division title at the time. Nobody gave us a ghost of a chance, and all we were determined to do was to go out at St James's Park and enjoy ourselves before a massive crowd. Then we scored with our first attack after just two minutes, when I managed to make the chance for Peter Henderson to round off.

We were under siege for the next hour or more, as Newcastle bombarded us with everything they could muster. They hit the bar, were foiled by desperate goal-line clearances – but they couldn't get

that elusive goal to equalize. Then, about twenty minutes from the
end, we broke away, Ron Phillips crossed and I just knocked it in
with my left foot. Our players went wild. You'd have thought we
were winning at Wembley as we celebrated. And we held on to our
2–0 lead to the end. What I recall to this day, though, is the
marvellous generosity of that Geordie crowd. They must have been
bitterly upset to see their team beaten like that, but they still
applauded us off the pitch. I have labelled them the best supporters
in England ever since that game. And I have never had any reason
to change that opinion. I am just delighted that Kevin Keegan has
built Newcastle into one of the country's great teams over the last
few seasons – those super fans deserve that.

   We went on to beat Millwall 2–0 in the fourth round, before
eventually seeing our dreams come to an end when we lost 2–1 at
Ipswich in the following round. But I had already collected my FA
Cup bonus – my very first car, which I bought with the £150 bonus
we received for beating Millwall. It wasn't much, an old Avenger
that wasn't a very reliable starter. But I was the proudest boy in Flint
as I drove it around the town. My wages had also gone up by then,
to a basic fifty pounds a week. With bonuses I could earn around
eighty pounds, staggering rewards for a youngster who had learned
the value of a pound note. Unemployment was rife in the area as the
steelworks and the factories closed. My own brothers, some of them
on the dole, had to scrimp and scrape to make ends meet. I truly
appreciated how fortunate I was, being so well paid to do a job I
loved.

   It was around this time that I met Tracy, who was to become my
wife seven years later. And the old hell-raising Ian Rush really was
becoming a thing of the past. My career came first and foremost
now, and the only time I had a drink was on Saturday nights after a
game. But I was happy with my life, seeing the next ten years ahead
of me with Chester. Quite honestly, my ambitions stretched no

further at that time. There had been speculation in the newspapers that bigger clubs were eyeing my progress, but I took little notice. Until the day, that is, when Alan Oakes called me into his office to inform me that Liverpool wanted to sign me.

They wanted a quick answer because it was only a few days before the transfer deadline, so Oakes told me to go home and think about it overnight. I didn't lose much sleep at all. I decided, pretty quickly, that I would only be making a fool of myself if I went to one of the greatest clubs in Europe. I just wasn't in their class. I informed the manager the next day that I would prefer to stay with Chester and he seemed genuinely pleased. And I honestly thought that would be the end of any transfer talk. Manchester City, who had also enquired about me, had pulled out, believing I was not ready. And that didn't hurt me – it suited me quite well.

Now I could happily spend the rest of my playing days at Sealand Road. But a few weeks later, as we were returning on our coach from an away game, Alan Oakes came and sat beside me. 'Liverpool have made another offer for you,' he told me. Although I remained silent, he could sense that I was far from happy at the prospect. 'How much would you want to go there?' he asked me.

This was my opportunity to end the talk once and for all. 'I'd want at least a hundred quid a week,' I told him.

He erupted with laughter. 'Son, I'll pay you more than that if you're still with Chester next season,' he said.

A couple of days later I reluctantly agreed to go with Alan Oakes and my father to Anfield, where we met the Liverpool manager Bob Paisley. We were taken on a tour of their training ground, and then to Anfield, where we had lunch. It was all so imposing, so big and grand, that I had decided in my own mind that I ought to give it a go. Just being there made me excited. And my father was even more awe-struck than I was. Liverpool was his team, remember, and here he was exchanging small talk with the greatest manager in the country. We all sat down in Bob Paisley's office and Oakes asked him casually, 'How much would Ian earn for playing for Liverpool?'

The answer came equally calmly 'We'll pay him three hundred pounds a week...'

It was like being hit on the head by a gold bar! I was speechless for a few seconds, before I recovered sufficient composure to ask for a pen so that I could sign the contract on Paisley's desk. My father was as wide-eyed as I was. Although the transfer deadline had passed, I was able to play a couple of reserve games for Liverpool before the season ended. I was also given an emotional farewell at Chester, where double the normal crowd thronged the ground for my last game and hundreds of youngsters invaded the pitch at the end to cheer me off.

Making my goodbyes to the other players, and to people like Alan Oakes and Cliff Sear, was just as difficult. I knew I owed so much to both those men. It was Oakes who gave me one final piece of advice before I left. 'Just remember this,' he told me. 'Your first year at Liverpool will be the worst year of your life. There will be times you'll hate it so much you'll want to come running back here – or even pack the game in. You'll hate me for letting you go there. But you've got to stick at it, tough it out. Then you will have a wonderful career. I know you have the ability, otherwise I would not let you go. You've got to keep that same belief inside yourself.'

Frankly, I didn't take a lot of notice of Alan's words at the time. I was Britain's costliest ever teenager, with the £350,000 Liverpool were paying for me. I was about to earn a fortune – and I was going to play for the best team in Europe. Who needed advice?

Six months later, I was bitterly recalling every word of that warning. And wishing I'd never clapped eyes on Bob Paisley or Liverpool.

Chapter 3

Anfield Agony – and Ecstasy

Bob Paisley was the most successful manager in the whole history of English football. The fact that he was voted Manager of the Year six times in his nine seasons in charge at Liverpool is vivid testimony to his greatness. The Anfield trophy cabinet used to groan with the weight of all the silverware. There were those who feared for the future of the club when Bill Shankly, who had lifted them from the Second Division to the top of the First Division, retired in 1974. Yet Paisley, who had been his assistant, built a side that was the best in Europe, perhaps in the whole world. He was never one for being flash. I can barely remember seeing him when he wasn't dressed in his old cardigan, and his only abiding obsession in life – apart from Liverpool Football Club – was horse-racing. He spent more time studying *Sporting Life* than any dossiers he ever had on our opposition!

But the unassuming, almost grandfatherly façade disguised a brain that was as sharp as that of any eminent psychologist. Paisley was a master of mind-games, as well as possessing the most knowledgeable footballing brain I have ever known. The memories of his

genius came flooding back to me on 22 April 1996, when I
attended a memorial service for him at Liverpool Cathedral. When
Bob died a little bit earlier in the year, his widow Jessie requested
that the funeral should be a private, family affair. And the fans
respected her wishes. Such sad occasions are not for the world to
gawp at.

But the city wanted to pay its own respects to a man who had
helped to bring it so much glory. And I think that half the
population of Merseyside was crammed into the cathedral, and
standing outside, as Jessie and former Liverpool and England
winger Ian Callaghan did the readings. I was there, along with other
old Anfield favourites like Phil Thompson and Tommy Smith, and
even Everton old boys Colin Harvey and Graeme Sharpe were
among the congregation, which also, of course, included the entire
Liverpool staff and Joe Fagan, who succeeded Paisley. It was a day
to celebrate the memory of a man who had made such an
outstanding contribution to football and to the region.

I spent my first three years at Anfield under Paisley's
management. And I have to confess that for the first fifteen months
or so I couldn't stand him. In fact, I hated just about everything at
Liverpool in my first season there. But when I look back at it now,
I can smile at the way he used all those psychological wiles to steer
my career onto the right course. It all seemed so different at the
time, though. I was still a painfully shy eighteen-year-old rookie
when I joined Liverpool, still hardly believing that the best club in
Europe could be interested in me. I gave myself two years to see if
I could make it at Anfield. Otherwise, I would go back to Chester
and see out my career there.

I wasn't totally lacking in self-confidence when I started my first
proper season there in 1980–1. I had been called into the Welsh
squad for the British Championships at the end of the previous
season and was thrilled to make my international début, as second-

half substitute at Hampden Park when Ian Walsh was injured. But I certainly did not expect to walk straight into the Liverpool team. You had only to glance round the dressing room to see all the great players they had: Kenny Dalglish, Graeme Souness, Ray Clemence...they were so famous that I was scared even to talk to them. I used to be first to arrive for training every morning because I was frightened of being late. Then, when the senior players arrived, they would give me terrible stick because of the clothes I was wearing.

Dalglish would always lead the banter, muttering some wisecrack like, 'Been repairing the car, have you?' And that would start them all off. I guess I was a bit of a scruff. I'd just pull on a T-shirt and a pair of old jeans to wear to training. I didn't see the point of dressing up, just to hang the clothes on the dressing-room peg. But I didn't answer them back. I would force a totally false smile, but inside I was squirming. I hated them all. I couldn't wait to get out of the place, back home to where none of the lads dressed any differently from me.

It seems so juvenile and petty when I look back at it now. All they were doing was indulging in a bit of harmless banter, just as I have done with scores of younger players over the years. It's part of footballing life, and what you must not do is take offence. Professional football is a ruthless, demanding business. It involves a lot of physical pain and tremendous mental pressures. If you can't stand a bit of mickey-taking, how are you going to cope when your back's to the wall, with 60,000 frenzied supporters screaming and jeering at you in Milan or Barcelona?

I spent most of that season in the reserve team, which was winning the Central League for the second year in a row, while the senior team was battling through to the final of the League Cup and the semi-final of the European Cup. I did make my first-team début in a 1–1 draw at Ipswich in December 1980, when Dalglish had to

pull out through injury. But that was an isolated highlight. The rest
of the time I was feeling my way with the second team: a pretty
good side in its own right, with players like Steve Ogrizovic, Kevin
Sheedy, Alan Harper, Howard Gayle and Colin Irwin, who all went
on to have First Division careers elsewhere. There was a restless
edge to the team, though. Most of the lads knew deep down that
they were not going to make it at Anfield and were resigned to
moving on. I also felt that, in some quarters, there was a bit of
animosity towards me, because I had cost so much money.

Young players who had been at the club since leaving school
were envious, because Liverpool had splashed out to sign me,
which suggested that I had more of a future there than they did. I
didn't see it that way, mind you. I grew more and more miserable
and depressed as the season wore on. I scored only a dozen goals
for the reserves in the whole campaign. The funny thing was that I
knew I was playing quite well. It did not take me long to lose my
complex about not being good enough for Liverpool. By the spring
of my first season I really felt I had the ability. And Bob Paisley must
have spotted some potential in me, because I had a dramatic call to
play in the League Cup Final replay against West Ham when poor
David Johnson, who suffered so much from injury, had to pull out.

The sides had drawn 1–1 at Wembley – I'd gone along with the
rest of the reserves to watch from the stand. I still did not expect to
be involved in the replay, at Aston Villa's Villa Park ground on
Wednesday, 1 April 1981, even though I was in the squad. Steve
Heighway, who had been out himself through injury, was expected
to recover in time. But he pulled out on the morning of the game –
and I was in. Thankfully it wasn't an All Fools' Day ending for me
– we beat West Ham 2–1 after Paul Goddard had put them in front,
with Kenny Dalglish and Alan Hansen getting our goals.

I kept my place for the first leg of the European Cup semi-final
with Bayern Munich, which followed soon afterwards, and I was

sub for the return, with Johnson fit again. We reached the final on the away goals ruling, after drawing 0–0 at our place and then 1–1 in Germany. I ended the season playing in seven First Division games all told, as well as the League Cup Final replay and that game against Bayern. While I did not expect to win a starting place in the side for the European Cup Final against Real Madrid in Paris, Bob Paisley had assured me that I would be in the squad.

After all the trials and tribulations of the season, I was finally beginning to enjoy myself. I picked up an £800 bonus for helping to win the League Cup, while I was on a first-team win bonus of £250. Things were going so well financially that I was able to trade in my old banger for a brand-new car. And I was feeling much more confident and relaxed with the other players. Kenny Dalglish, whom I had disliked so much, was brilliant towards me. He was for ever giving me advice on the field, making me aware of situations, spotting weaknesses in the opposition defence, telling me when and how to make my runs off the ball.

And I had made my début at Wembley, coming on as a substitute for Wales in a goal-less draw against England. I was starting to believe I had cracked it ahead of the two-year timetable I had set myself.

There were eighteen players named in the party that flew to Paris the day before the European Cup Final, which meant that, with only five substitutes allowed, two were going to be unlucky. It didn't worry me unduly, because Paisley had promised me I would be involved. But on the morning of the game he gathered us all together and said, 'I'm going to have to disappoint two of you: Avi Cohen and...Ian Rush.' That was all he said. I was so stunned that I could not even bring myself to ask him why he had gone back on his word. It was one of the lowest points in my whole life.

Liverpool won the final 1–0, thanks to a cracking goal from left back Alan Kennedy. And I was genuinely pleased for the players.

But I was in no mood to join the celebrations. I joined Ronnie Whelan and Kevin Sheedy, two of my mates in the reserve team, and we had our own private party well away from the official one. I did not even join the players on the coach that took them on a triumphant journey through Liverpool when the party flew back from Paris the following day. I was gutted.

But Roy Evans, who was then Liverpool's reserve team trainer, helped to lift my spirits when he told me a few days later, 'You've got the ability to walk into the first team. It's all down to how much you want it – but I'll be expecting to see you there regularly next season.' I still spent that summer nursing a simmering resentment towards Paisley, however. And the festering bitterness inside me burst into open rage at the start of the new season, 1981–2. We were playing in a pre-season tournament on the Continent in preparation for the new campaign, and all the players were sitting round the dinner table when the topic of conversation turned towards money. Although I had committed myself to a three-year contract when I signed, the other players told me that I would get a big wage increase because I had established myself in the first-team squad. 'You'll get at least a hundred pounds a week rise,' they said.

Whether they were just winding me up is something I do not know to this very day. I was determined to see the manager as soon as we arrived home to make my claim. In the event, Bob Paisley was first to act, calling me into his office to tell me, 'I'm going to give you a ten per cent rise.'

That meant only thirty pounds on top of my previous £300, so I told him, 'I think I've earned more than that. I want a hundred pounds a week. I think I've done well for you in my first season.'

He reflected for a few moments, then agreed with me.

'So why won't you give me a better rise?' I asked, beginning to raise my voice in anger.

'It's simple enough – you've got to prove yourself first, you've got to get into the side regularly.' He gave me two weeks to think things over, but by now I was determined to stick to my guns.

I can be a stubborn so-and-so when I put my mind to it. I told him I was not prepared to accept the offer and he said simply, 'That's okay. It's your decision.' We did not exchange another word, but I was not in the side that started the season. Instead I was back in the reserves. Mark Lawrenson, who had only just joined us from Brighton, was in the senior team along with Bruce Grobbelaar, who had arrived at Anfield after me, which left me feeling even more isolated. With hindsight, I can see that money was by no means the root of the problem. I had not forgiven Paisley for that European Cup Final disappointment and I was using the pay-offer as an excuse to show my anger.

Frankly, my wage packet has never been the all-important thing for me, right the way through my career. I'm not stupid, I like to have enough money to be able to live more than comfortably, but that came along as a natural accompaniment to my career as it developed. If someone offered me the choice between winning £1,000 or scoring a vital goal, the goal would always be the winner. But at this stage I guess my mind was not focusing all that sensibly. Eventually, after spending all morning building up my courage, I went back in to see Paisley. 'What's happening? Why have you left me out of the side? I played in the pre-season games but you've left me out now. Why?' I blurted out.

His reply was direct – and pretty damning. 'You're not worth your place. You are supposed to be a centre forward but you're not scoring goals,' he said.

'I thought football was supposed to be a team game,' I shouted back at him, my temper beginning to rise.

Paisley remained calm, but told me in no uncertain terms, 'That's your trouble. I've watched you in matches and in training, and all you ever want to do is to lay the ball off all the time. You're afraid to take responsibility on your own shoulders.'

That really riled me. 'I've been taught ever since I came here that football is all about retaining possession. You're not supposed to give the bloody ball away, are you?' I yelled.

'Your trouble is that you're frightened to think for yourself. As a centre forward, your main job in the team is to score goals. But you haven't scored a single goal for us yet. That's why you're not playing.'

'I can score goals,' I shouted back.

'Well, why in hell's name aren't you, then? Your trouble is that you're not showing the instinct of a natural goal-scorer. There are times when you have to adopt a selfish attitude. It might be a team game, but when you have the goal in your sights you have to think only about yourself.'

By this stage I was furious. 'If you think like that about me, there's no point in me staying here then,' I yelled.

Paisley suddenly lowered his own voice to little more than a whisper. 'Are you saying you want to go? If that's what you want, you can leave. What do you want?' he asked me.

So that was it! He didn't even want me to stay. 'All right, I'll go. You can stick your club!' I told him, as I got up to leave his office.

As I was opening the door, he fired a parting shot. 'We bought you to score goals for us. Why don't you go out there and prove you can do that?'

By now I was at boiling point. 'I'll show you I can bloody well score goals!' I shouted as I closed the door.

And that was that. I was closing the door not only on the manager but on Liverpool Football Club. As far as I was concerned, I was on the transfer list. I would be with a new club before long. I was grimly determined to prove to this man that I was a natural, instinctive goal-scorer. But I did not expect to be proving it with

Liverpool. My plan was to score so regularly in the reserve side that other clubs would be bound to take notice – and want me to join them. From now on I was going to be the most selfish, ruthless striker you could imagine. To hell with the rest of the team. All I was going to concentrate on was scoring goals.

The plan worked, too. I scored six goals in five games in the Central League. I knew I was not playing particularly well overall, but I was doing the job I was there for. Speculation started in the newspapers that Crystal Palace were closely monitoring my progress. I was delighted. Selhurst Park in London was a long way away, but I was ready to uproot myself from my family if the chance came. Palace, under Terry Venables, were then being hailed as the 'Team of the Eighties' and I had a couple of friends there from the Welsh squad, Peter Nicholas and Ian Walsh. Bob Paisley had told me he was ready to let me go. A year or more of strife and toil was coming to an end. All I wanted was a fresh start.

While I was working off my frustrations in the reserves, however, the first team had not started the season particularly well. They had won only two of their opening seven games and were finding it far from easy to score goals. I was on the substitutes' bench against OPS Oulu, an amateur team from Finland, in the European Cup and came on late in the game to score in our 7–0 win. It was my first goal for Liverpool – a simple tap-in – but it did not raise any great joy inside me. Frankly, the Finns would have struggled to beat our reserve side. Then, when the luckless David Johnson was injured yet again, I played a full game in the League Cup against Exeter and scored twice – the first goal a real cracker with my left foot from thirty yards, as good as any I ever scored for Liverpool since.

Even with such stars as Kenny Dalglish, Graeme Souness and Terry McDermott around me, I was still determined to be as selfish and single-minded as I had been in the reserves. If I had the ball and could even sniff the opposition goal, that's where I would head for. If the big names around me were upset, that was their problem. I was still playing for a move, and my own future was all that mattered to me. Bob Paisley did not utter a word of praise to me after my double against Exeter, so obviously his views had not changed. He must have been satisfied, though, because I kept my place in the team for the next game – at home to Leeds.

With all due respect to Oulu and Exeter, this was a totally different proposition. Leeds were our great northern rivals at the time, and there was a lot of pride at stake. There was a tension in our dressing room that I had never experienced before, and even the hardened old pros around me were keyed up. Nearly 36,000 people were packed into Anfield. And for them and for me it was to be an afternoon to savour. We won 3–0...and I scored twice. Both in front of the Kop, as well, in the first half. I can recall those goals vividly to this very day.

The first came when I hurled myself at a bouncing cross to reach it just before the Leeds goalkeeper John Lukic, and steer it past him into the net. The Kop exploded – and I was as delirious as any of them. I have scored hundreds of goals since, but I still find it impossible to explain the surge of emotion you get at a moment like that. I saw the goals on television later, and I could hardly believe it was me who was running along the front of the Kop with all the wildness of a headless chicken. I guess it must be some kind of overflowing adrenalin that causes it, but scoring a vital goal in a big game, with tens of thousands of supporters screaming their joy...the ecstasy becomes delirium. It's like floating on air. Quite simply, it's the most wonderful feeling in the world.

Thankfully, I'm not alone when it comes to goal-scoring celebrations. I've seen players become so hysterical that they burst into tears. It is an emotional release from the tension and the pressure that build up inside you in the approach to a game. It lasts no more than a few seconds, before reality floods back and then you have to concentrate again on the match in hand. There have been moves from FIFA over the last few years to curtail such celebrations, and some referees have become somewhat heavy-handed in administering the law, even showing yellow cards to those indulging in over-joyous festivities. But I feel it would be a sad day if we saw such emotional outpourings outlawed, as some critics would like. You might as well ask the supporters to refrain from making too much noise when their team scores!

I scored my second about twenty minutes later, getting in first to a low cross and then steering past Lukic from a narrow angle. Suddenly the fans on the Kop were chanting my name – I was their hero of the afternoon. The rest of the game went by in a blur, Trevor Cherry scoring into his own net in the second half to complete our victory. Then I had the press and the crowds of back-slappers to contend with – the worst ordeal of the afternoon for someone who was still painfully shy. I uttered a few platitudes about my performance, but I did not reveal my true feelings. I still did not see any long-term future for myself at Anfield.

Kenny Dalglish, who had been a real inspiration to me on the pitch, was among the first to shake my hand at the end. All the other players and our coaches, Joe Fagan and Ronnie Moran, added their congratulations. But from Paisley there was not a word. Just a general 'well done' to all the players, but nothing at all to me. There were no stars or favourites as far as he was concerned. The team had won, not just the kid who scored a couple of goals. I was disappointed at the time, but looking back I can understand his attitude.

Paisley was in charge of the greatest club in Europe – and some of the greatest players in the whole world. Yet genuine superstars like Dalglish and Souness were treated no differently from the rest. There was no room for prima donnas. This had always been the case under Bill Shankly, and Paisley saw no reason to change it.

And I began to understand his philosophy as the weeks went by and I retained my place in the team. Merely by selecting me he was showing his confidence in my ability. And as the goals continued to flow and I grew in confidence, I began to enjoy myself more with every game. By Christmas 1981 I had really established myself in the team, and the last thing in the world I wanted right then was to leave.

Then the boss called me into his office after training one day and told me, 'We feel you've earned the hundred-pound-a-week pay-rise you asked for now.' It was the peace-pipe that he was offering.

But I was still a trifle sore about the way he had originally turned me down. So I think I surprised him when I answered, 'I'm not sure I want to sign a new contract. I'll have to think it over.' A week or so later, I went back to him and said, 'I want the hundred pounds a week extra, plus the ten per cent you offered me.' I wasn't being greedy, I just felt there was a point of principle at stake.

He turned me down at first, but called me back into his office a few days later and said that the club had agreed to my demand. I felt I had scored a little victory of some sort. But I reckon he had a much bigger last laugh than I did.

Looking back now, I don't believe it was ever Paisley's intention to sell me, despite all my doubts and worries. I think he had looked at my character and decided that the way to get the best out of me was to make me angry. That's why he gave me that lecture about not scoring enough goals. He was a genius when it came to human nature, just as much as he was a genius about football. And he had used that psychological weapon to make me do exactly what he wanted me to do. The more I watched him over the next two years before he retired, the more I had to admire him.

Bob Paisley was never the easiest person to talk to, being a quiet and introverted man. But he knew just about everything when it came to dealing with the players. He knew how to manipulate all of them in different ways. We never mentioned that contract row again. And though I went on to score sixty goals in those seasons before he left, he never once singled me out for special praise. Not that I ever expected it by that stage. I knew he was happy with me, because I kept my place in the team. That was what really mattered.

After that uncertain start to the season, the team was really flying as well. We hit a sensational spell, winning eleven games in a row to emerge without a single defeat from our last sixteen games as we retained the League Championship and lifted the League Cup at Wembley, beating Tottenham Hotspur 3–1 after extra time. That was my first Wembley final and a real highlight. It also brought me my first record in senior football. I had scored seven goals on our march to the final, to equal the existing League Cup record. Just one more would beat it – and Wembley! What an arena to achieve it. I had played there once, as a substitute for twenty minutes with Wales, but this was a huge occasion for me.

All that week building up to the final, the atmosphere and the tension increased at Anfield, before we finally left for London on the Friday. I normally enjoy a long lie-in on match-days, but this time I could barely sleep. Ronnie Whelan, my room-mate, was just as keyed up, so we went down for breakfast long before anyone else. The excitement reached fever pitch when we arrived at the stadium and walked out to get an early feel of the place. All I could see were masses of red-and-white-bedecked supporters on one side, navy-blue-and-white on the other. Because the stadium is so vast and the crowds so far away from the playing surface, you don't feel the same tightness as at normal grounds. At Anfield, for example, you can almost reach out and touch the spectators.

I know that I had already collected a winner's medal in the competition the year before, but even that excitement, wonderful though it was at the time, bore no comparison to my feelings right now. A Cup Final at Wembley is something unique, different from anything else in the game, something you cherish for ever. It's not so much a football match as an Event...and it whistles by in a blur. Mind you, this particular game sped by far too quickly for my liking. Steve Archibald had given Spurs a first-half lead and, despite our mounting second-half pressure, time was virtually up – and we were still trailing.

Then my mate Ronnie Whelan, playing the game of his life, scrambled the equalizer with just seconds left. Sheer ecstasy! We went wild with delight, because I think we all knew then that the trophy was ours. You only had to look at the total dejection on the faces of the Spurs players to see how mentally shattered they were. They had no fight left in them and we dominated the half-hour of extra time. Whelan, who seemed to be running more feverishly with every passing minute, put us in front with his second goal.

And then, a couple of minutes from the end, David Johnson, who had come on in place of Terry McDermott, made a great run down our left, cut inside to draw out Ray Clemence, then laid the ball back for me to score as easy a goal as I've ever had. Suddenly any tiredness in my legs vanished. I was sprinting round Wembley like a two-year-old, so feverishly excited by scoring a goal and breaking the record that my mind went totally blank. To this day I can't remember a thing about the rest of the game, or even the presentation afterwards. I don't even know who gave me my medal!

I only started functioning again back in the dressing room, with the noise deafening, as everyone at the club – the reserves, the back-room staff, even the directors – joined in the celebrations. Then we had a triumphant home-coming the next day, with thousands upon thousands of fans lining the streets to wave their scarves and banners and cheer us every inch of the way to Anfield. Liverpool being what it is, though, there wasn't too much time for celebration. We still had a League Championship trophy to win. Our tremendous form in the second half of the season had taken us to the top of the table, but Ipswich were pushing us hard. We could afford to take nothing for granted, but we kept on winning until we reached the point where we needed to beat Tottenham – again! – in our last home game to be sure of taking the title. We had the cushion of a final away game at Middlesbrough, but we badly wanted to win the trophy before our own supporters.

Anfield was filled to overflowing, but for a long while it looked as though the supporters were going to be left deflated. Glenn Hoddle scored with a brilliant drive to put Spurs ahead and, with Clemence in inspirational form on his old home ground, they held out until the last half-hour. But then we finally broke their resistance with three quick goals from Mark Lawrenson, Kenny Dalglish and Ronnie Whelan. The League Championship trophy was ours again, just as it had been four times in the previous six seasons. But this was a first for me, an incredible way to end my initial season in the senior team.

It was a very different kind of emotion from the fever-pitch excitement of Wembley. I remember sitting for quite a while in the dressing room, just looking back on what Liverpool had achieved, and on what I had achieved in my short time there. You get a kind of inner glow that comes from the satisfaction of proving yourselves the best team in the hardest league in the world. I've never had an inflated opinion of myself, but I felt so proud at that moment that I was almost ready to burst. I understood now what the older players had so often said – that winning the League is the greatest honour of all.

A few days later, I learned that other great maxim...that footballers, and Liverpool footballers in particular, enjoy a drink! With the title won, the squad was already in festive mood as we drove up to the North-East to play Middlesbrough on the following Tuesday night. We didn't even leave Anfield until the morning of the game, which shows that we weren't taking it too seriously. When we checked into our hotel, one or two of the senior players suggested that we go out for an afternoon stroll. I joined them, thinking the fresh air would do me good. But we got no further than the first pub. Suddenly there was a glass of lager shoved in front of me, then another, then several more.

After a couple of hours I was in convivial mood, to say the least. So were the rest of the team, all seated with me. It was party time – and our game was only a few hours away! I'd never done anything like this so close to a match before. We had to dash back to the hotel to dive into bed before four o'clock, when our trainer Ronnie Moran would be checking the rooms to make sure that we were all sleeping peacefully. We made it with five minutes to spare – although I'm not sure that Ronnie was ever really taken in. He must have smelled the booze every time he opened a bedroom door! I had no more than half an hour's sleep, and felt like grim death when I woke up. I played like it, too. I recall Graeme Souness sidling over to me and giving me a right ear-bashing. 'You are allowed to kick the ball, you know!' he said.

Poor Middlesbrough, who had already been relegated, must have wondered what kind of Fred Karno's Army they were up against. Apparently their players had heard about our afternoon escapade, so they were a little bit embarrassed about facing us. The game finished without a goal – without a real tackle, come to that. And I'm not proud of what happened. I understand that supporters pay out good money to watch games and at least deserve to see players trying to give their all. But footballers are only human, and we have our weaknesses just like everyone else. Believe me, there has never been a more ruthlessly professional bunch of players than that lot.

If the game had actually counted for anything, even if Boro could have stayed up by beating us, we would have been up for it.

But with absolutely nothing at stake, and at the end of a long, gruelling season, with the title already in our hands, we let our hair down. We shouldn't have done so, I know. But if nobody ever made the odd mistake in this life, it would be a dull old world, wouldn't it?

I ended that first season with thirty goals all told – seventeen in the League, eight in the League Cup, three in the FA Cup and a couple in Europe. I was pleased with my contribution, but I knew I was still very much a novice and had a long, long way to go to become a good player. I knew it meant I had to be more than just a goal-scorer. I had to concentrate on playing for the team. And I like to think that I had become a much more effective all-round player by the following season, 1982–3, when I scored thirty goals again – twenty-four in the League this time – and Liverpool completed another League Championship and Milk Cup (the League Cup's new name) double.

I felt far more relaxed and established in the first team that year – and what a season we had. Watford were our nearest rivals, but we had the title sewn up by Easter and eventually finished a massive eleven points ahead of them. I missed seven games of our run-in after suffering a groin injury. But I did have some memorable moments, with hat-tricks against Coventry and Notts County, and an even sweeter Saturday afternoon against our old enemies Everton...at Goodison Park, too! I had gone half-a-dozen games without a goal when we played them, in November. When a young player hits a lean spell, it invariably starts a murmur that perhaps he wasn't as good as his potential had suggested. But I had one of those blessed afternoons when every touch I made, every shot I had, came off. I finished up scoring four times in our 5–0 victory – and Everton's shell-shocked goalkeeper was my Welsh team-mate Neville Southall! Poor Nev was so overwhelmed by it all that he was left out of Everton's next game and did not win his place back for more than four months.

We'd gone to the top of the table just a week before that game – and we stayed there for the next six months, losing only one League game in the last twenty-seven. Without ever feeling complacent, we used to feel well nigh unbeatable – and our record proved that we were. Going back to Wembley was another fantastic occasion. The older lads in the side used to say that once you've played in a final there, it only whets your appetite to go back, and it was true. To make it even more memorable, we played our bitter Lancashire rivals, Manchester United.

It was almost a repeat of twelve months before. United scored in the first half through Norman Whiteside, but we battered them after the break to get an equalizer through Alan Kennedy. That took the game to extra time – when Ronnie Whelan scored the winner for us. But I learned another truism about Wembley that afternoon. The playing surface is so lush that it does sap your stamina, especially when you've put everything into the ninety minutes and then you have to go through the ordeal of an extra half-hour. I was knackered in the final minutes, when I suddenly felt a bit of a twinge in my groin.

I didn't give it much thought at the time. But by the next morning I could barely move my legs, the pain was so intense. The players were staying down in London, with our wives and girlfriends, so that we could attend the Professional Footballers' Association Annual Dinner, so I just went for a dip in the pool of the hotel where we were staying to see if that would ease the stiffness. It seemed to help, so I was quite relaxed by the evening. And what a night it turned out to be for Liverpool. We had heard that Kenny Dalglish was in line to win the PFA Player of the Year award, and that's why we were all determined to be there, to support him.

We were in the middle of the meal when Graeme Souness came back to report to us that Kenny had indeed won the award – and that I had been voted Young Player of the Year, to complete a glorious double honour for the club. It was a stunning moment for me. To be chosen by all the other players in the country after only two full seasons in the First Division was a tremendous accolade – but I froze when I realized that I would have to make a speech in front of all those hundreds of people. I stopped eating and just hit the wine bottle instead, looking for instant Dutch courage. Then I looked across the table at Kenny, and he seemed just as edgy as I was. He was one of the greatest players in the world, and I'd never seen him show fear against the most intimidating defenders, in front of hostile crowds. But right now he had gone pale with stage-fright.

Fortunately, the presentations were being made by Mike England, the Welsh manager. That certainly helped me to relax a bit as I received my trophy. 'Thanks, Dad!' I said to him, pulling his leg, because he had been saying so many nice things about me in the past couple of years that the other lads in the Welsh team used to claim that he was my father. My little joke raised a few laughs among those watching, and I mumbled a few other words before sitting down again. I really did feel honoured – I even came third in the main award, which Kenny won. And just to prove how high Liverpool's standing was among their fellow-professionals, Graeme Souness and Mark Lawrenson were also voted into the top six.

But my groin was still hurting when I arrived home the next day. It was the first real injury I had ever suffered and I didn't know how to cope with it at all. I had treatment, which took the soreness away, enabling me to play for a couple of games, but then it became so painful that I had to give it a good long rest. I wasn't too unhappy, because we had already wrapped up the League – something we dearly wanted to do for Bob Paisley, who had announced that he was retiring at the end of the season. It says much for the stability of the club that his decision, though it left the players saddened, did not cause a single ripple of apprehension.

In any other club there would have been waves of unrest at the departure of a man who had stamped himself as one of the greatest managers – possibly the greatest manager – of all time by winning six League Championships in nine years, as well as three League Cups, three European Cups and the UEFA Cup once. The only trophy that eluded him was the FA Cup. Souness, the club captain, made a marvellous gesture on behalf of all the players when he insisted that Paisley walked up to the Royal Box at Wembley after the Milk Cup Final to collect the trophy.

But his leaving meant that another member of the famous Bootroom, or the back-room staff, Joe Fagan, would simply step up to take his place, in the way Paisley had when Bill Shankly announced his retirement. It was the Liverpool way. Nothing would change, apart from the fact that we would now have to get used to calling Fagan 'Gaffer' instead of Joe. Why change a winning formula, a recipe that had brought so much enduring success to the club over the past twenty years? I certainly had no fears as the season ended on another triumphant note for me, when I won the Robinsons Barley Water Young Player of the Season award. The prize was a spanking new car – which wasn't much use to me right then, because I'd been banned from driving after being caught speeding three times!

The season did have its spectacular finale for me, though...a right royal punch-up among half a dozen of the younger players! It happened on our end-of-season trip to Israel, where we were due to play a local team in Tel Aviv. The night before the game a bunch of us went out to enjoy ourselves at an open bar in a lovely square in the city. We were all pretty high, and I was as drunk as anybody in the company. I vaguely recall being suddenly shoved in the back, which caused me to lurch forward and crash to the floor. David Hodgson, who had joined us from Middlesbrough, had become a good pal of mine – we used to travel to training together – and he was up in arms at what happened.

'Who did that? Who pushed my mate Rushy over?' he was yelling. By the time I climbed unsteadily to my feet, Hodgy and Ronnie Whelan were grappling. The next thing I knew, pandemonium had broken out, with Hodgy and me taking on the rest. It must have looked like a scene from a second-rate spaghetti western, with chairs and tables being overturned and bottles and glasses flying. Alan Kennedy, who was a bit more sober than the rest of us, tried to break it up – and copped a black eye for his pains! He dived in to prevent John McGregor from thumping me, and caught a punch himself.

By the next morning, the whole affair had become the biggest belly-laugh in years, especially for the older players, who took the mickey out of us unmercifully. But Bob Paisley had naturally got to know that something untoward had happened. He rounded us up and asked us, 'Right, you lot, who's been fighting?' Kennedy was by now sporting a lovely black eye, I had a big gash on the side of my face...so the evidence was pretty overwhelming. But we all told him, 'Not us, boss,' and, after muttering a few well-chosen words, he walked away, still shaking his head. No further action was taken, after we had a whip-round to pay for the damage. But I wonder to this day if Paisley was half-relieved that it was his final match in charge!

Chapter 4

The High Road to Hell

Goals have been my life-blood for as long as I can remember. I crave them, I eat them up as greedily as a starving man would wolf down a meal. If I'm not scoring goals, my whole family suffers, my whole mood darkens. As you get older and – so they say! – wiser, you at least learn to accept that life has its down-side as well as its up, that there are going to be lows as well as highs. But on the basis that goals have always been my main business, the season of 1983–4 has to go down as the greatest of my life. I struck forty-nine goals – forty-seven for Liverpool and a couple for Wales – to win the Golden Boot as the top scorer in all Europe. The total reaches fifty if you count the goal I scored in the penalty shoot-out in the European Cup Final.

It was a fantastic campaign, as Liverpool won a unique treble – the League Championship, the Milk Cup and the European Cup. I broke the age-old scoring record for a single season at Liverpool, which was held by the legendary Roger Hunt, who once managed forty-two. I was voted Player of the Year by both the PFA and the

Football Writers' Association. The goals and the glory rolled in like a never-ending tide. Yet it was a season that had started with real problems for me – and ended with me seeing a million quid disappear into thin air.

That groin injury I had suffered towards the end of the previous season had nagged away at me all summer. I was able to complete the general fitness part of our pre-season training without too much trouble, but twisting and turning in our warm-up games was causing me real pain and anxiety. I wasn't very happy about playing in the Charity Shield game against Manchester United, but our new manager Joe Fagan persuaded me to. 'The only way we'll find out how serious it is, is for you to give it a real go,' he said. 'It's no use just messing about. If the groin's gone, you'll just have to rest it for the next three or four months.'

The new boss was already proving himself a pretty sharp mind-reader. 'We figured that the injury was mainly in your own mind. Because you'd never been injured before, it got to you, made you feel it was something far more serious than it actually was,' our coach Ronnie Moran told me some time later. They were right. I got through the game with no discomfort, although I felt I was some way below my best. So were Liverpool, come to that. We lost 2–0, and already the critics were sharpening their knives, writing us off. I started the season well enough, with four goals in our first half-dozen games. But then the goals dried up for four games – the longest run without one that I was to suffer all season.

It all came right, however, in a home game against Luton in October, when I had one of those golden days when everything came off. I scored five goals – the most I have ever struck in a professional match – and we hammered them 6–0 to move to the top of the table. Apart from a couple of odd weekends, we were never knocked off that position. I went on to score four against Coventry, hit a hat-trick against Aston Villa...I just couldn't stop the habit, not that I ever wanted to! I even scored with a dozen headers – and that's supposed to be my weakest area!

I finished with thirty-two League goals, and Dalglish was the second-highest scorer with seven. Yet he was more responsible than anyone for my success, and must have made well over half my goals. We had an almost telepathic understanding. I would make a run, knowing instinctively that he would find me with an inch-perfect pass. And although he had lost a little bit of his pace with the advancing years, he was still on the spot to snatch vital goals when we most needed them.

For Joe Fagan, it was a remarkable way to launch his managerial career. We didn't lose half a dozen games all season. When we did slip up, mind you, he could be vicious, and he used to get far angrier than I ever saw Bob Paisley. And Fagan wasn't bothered by reputations, either. Dalglish and Souness would be blasted in the dressing room just as much as the youngest player, if the boss felt they were out of line. But it was Craig Johnston, the Aussie we signed from Middlesbrough, who used to take more flak than anyone. Craig's problem was that he was a chatter-box, he just couldn't keep his mouth closed even if we'd just lost a game.

I got to understand Fagan well enough just to get in a corner and keep my head down after a bad performance. But it must be the Aussie inside Craig that made him such a bouncy character. He always felt he had played well, no matter what the result. I vividly remember the scene after we had lost 1–0 at home to Wolves, probably our worst performance of the season. Fagan was in an absolutely foul mood. 'You!' he roared at Johnston, 'you're always telling me when you've played well. Tell me when you've played badly.'

Craig couldn't resist answering back. 'I didn't think I was that bad, boss,' he said.

'You were bloody useless! You reminded me of that Road

Runner on the television, charging about like a headless chicken.'

I just kept my head down, knowing I had to look crestfallen, but almost exploding with laughter. I didn't dare make a sound, in case it became a huge belly-laugh. Goodness knows what Fagan would have done to me then!

We had a difficult run through to the Milk Cup Final, being taken to three games to put out Fulham and also needing replays to get past Birmingham and Sheffield Wednesday. But we eventually made it to Wembley to produce the Mersey dream final – Liverpool versus Everton. I doubt if the old stadium has ever known an afternoon quite like it. It was almost like a huge family party, with red and blue colours mingled together all round the place, without the slightest hint of trouble. If only football could always be like this.

That's not to say there was no tension surrounding the game. Everton were beginning to establish themselves as a real footballing power, and they were ready to challenge our position at the summit of the game – in fact, they were to go on to win the League title twice in the following three seasons. So there was a lot of local pride at stake. All through the week leading up to the final, fans would come up to us and beg us, 'You've gotta beat Everton – I won't be able to show my face at work next week if you don't!'

Despite the rivalry among the fans, the players from the two clubs have always mixed together pretty well socially. Merseyside is not that big a place, so I often met up with their lads for a drink. And two of their players, Neville Southall and Kevin Ratcliffe, were pals from the Welsh team. Kevin, in fact, was my room-mate for years with Wales, and one of my best friends in the game. But there's precious little room for friendship amid the hurly-burly of a Cup Final. We were in direct opposition, too, which added even more spice to the occasion. To be truthful, I never liked having him up against me, because he was the fastest defender in the First Division – and he knew just how I operated.

He hit me hard, twice, early in the game, grinning as I crashed to the ground. So when we went up together for a high cross, I just happened to catch him right on the nose with my arm. I hit him a bit harder than I meant to, though, and the next thing I knew his nose was bleeding, he was coughing up blood and having difficulty breathing. When he eventually got his breath back, he charged towards me – and we both burst out laughing! It was an illustration of how peculiar it can sometimes be when pals are caught on opposite sides. The game finished without a goal, which meant that everybody in the crowd could go home happy. But our supporters had the last laugh, when Graeme Souness scored the only goal of the replay. I stayed down in London after the first game to collect my PFA award the following night. Neil Kinnock presented the trophy, and I could see his eyes light up when I said how proud I was to be the first Welshman to win the award.

Kinnock may have been the leader of the Labour Party, but when it comes to sport he's a Welsh Nationalist through and through! We had a good long chat in the bar later and I was surprised how much he knew about sport – Welsh sport in particular. It was a special weekend for me, because on the train back to Liverpool the following morning I met Billy Liddell, one of the club's greatest players of all time. He regaled me with tales of the past, especially when the likes of Bob Paisley and Ronnie Moran were playing.

When that season ended we had become the first team since the war to win the League Championship three years in a row. And with a similar hat-trick in the Milk Cup, it was a vivid illustration of how great was our dominance of the domestic game. But the biggest thrill for me came in the European Cup. I was still finding my feet in Europe and we had crashed out early the two previous seasons, losing to CSKA Sofia of Bulgaria and then to the Polish side Widzew Lodz. It was a totally different world from the one back home, with man-markers, sweepers and a very different interpretation of the rules.

Most Continental referees allowed defenders to get away with the kind of obstruction that would never be tolerated in Britain. Yet firm but fair tackles were invariably blown up as fouls. The older players, like Dalglish and Souness, would always be there to encourage me and offer advice, but it's only with experience that you learn the arts and crafts of playing on different stages, in distant countries. We had a tough battle in the second round, being held 0–0 at home by Atletico Bilbao, only to squeeze home 1–0 in the away leg – I scored with a header. I headed home a couple more in the quarter-final, too, as we swept past Benfica.

That took us to the semi-final, where we were drawn to play Dynamo Bucharest. Having gone out to teams from Eastern Europe the two previous seasons, we were determined this would not happen again – but we had to endure two of the most brutal games I have ever played in to get through to the final. The Romanians clogged and kicked us so much in the first leg at Anfield that we seemed to spend most of the game leaping to avoid tackles that could have caused broken limbs. Even little Sammy Lee learned how to jump high that night – high enough to score the only goal with a header! But if that tie was bruising, the return two weeks later was enough to make your blood curdle. I needed eyes in the back of my head to see the boots come flying in at me, no matter where the ball happened to be. With 70,000 fans baying them on, the Romanian players just went wild. They were a disgrace to football that night.

But nobody could ever beat this Liverpool team by intimidation. We could take care of ourselves all right. Could you ever imagine players like Souness, Kennedy and Dalglish backing down from a fight? It was Souness, rallying his troops like a sergeant major, who made the opening for me to score in the first half – my one-hundredth goal for Liverpool, and as sweet as any I've ever struck. Dynamo pulled a goal back just before half-time, but our defence kept them at bay throughout the second half and I sneaked in with a second goal just before the end, to make sure of our passage through.

We were already singing and celebrating by the time we reached our dressing room – only for a sudden silence to descend on us as Joe Fagan walked in, looking as crestfallen as if we'd lost. He went slowly to the middle of the room and then, with his eyes staring at the floor, said quietly, 'I've got just one thing to say to you lot...' Then he leapt into the air, screaming, 'Yippee!' His act was brilliant – but it was so typical of a man who always wore his heart on his sleeve. If Fagan could be a ruthless taskmaster, he could also celebrate as wildly as any of his players.

Roma were our opponents in the final. And, as luck would have it, the game had already been designated to be played in their own home ground, the Olympic Stadium. It didn't seem right to me to allow one team to have such an overwhelming advantage. I often wonder what the Italians would have done if the final had been scheduled to take place at Anfield! But Liverpool did not raise any official objection. 'We'll just have to go and beat them in their own back yard,' said Fagan. When we arrived in Rome, though, I had my first experience of how fanatical a footballing nation the Italians are.

For some time there had been stories in the newspapers at home that Italian clubs were interested in me. Although I was flattered, I did not take too much interest at first, because I had just signed a new contract at Liverpool that was worth £500,000 over four years, provided the club remained at the top. For a lad of twenty-two, who five years before had been grateful to be earning twenty pounds a week, it was a fortune beyond my wildest dreams. I had no thoughts of ever leaving Liverpool – all I wanted to do was carry on scoring goals for them and keep winning trophies. Looking back now, I believe that Liverpool tied me to the contract eighteen months before my old one was up because they themselves had heard whispers of the Italian interest and were determined to keep me. I'm not blaming them for that – it's the job of a club to keep the players it regards as most important.

But the fact that officially I wasn't available didn't seem to bother the Italians at all – particularly the journalists, who mobbed me from the time I stepped out of the plane at Rome airport. And supporters who besieged the airport and our hotel were just as eager to ask when I was coming, and who I was joining. I couldn't tell them a thing, of course, because there was nothing to tell. But that didn't stop the newspapers from carrying banner headlines about me. I couldn't help being impressed, as well as amused, by such fanatical interest. Those few days were enough to convince me that Italy was the most passionate football country in Europe, if not the world.

And the atmosphere at the stadium for the final was unbelievable. Fireworks and smoke-bombs exploded around the ground, and we were struck by a barrage of coins and stones as we walked out from the dressing room. But we had talked about the hostility and intimidation we would be facing. We were ready for it and I don't think it affected us at all. If anything, it put us even more on our mettle. Every man-jack in the team ran his heart out that night to prevent the Italians from being able to settle into their rhythm. We silenced the whole ground when Phil Neal fired us ahead. And although Roma equalized just before half-time, they never seriously threatened to take over the game. It was stalemate after extra time, which meant that a penalty shoot-out would decide the destiny of the European Cup.

Now that's not a solution that appeals to me. I still believe that some provision should be made for a replay of such prestigious events, rather than the lottery we were about to face. Even playing on until one team finally scores would be a fairer way than this. But rules are rules – and at least both teams have to face the same nerve-racking tension. We hadn't even given a thought before the game about who our five penalty-takers should be. So we hastily organized it among ourselves. Graeme Souness, Phil Neal, Alan Kennedy, Steve Nicol and I were the five nominated.

We went first – and Nicol missed. But after Roma had scored with their first penalty and then Souness safely tucked one away for us, they missed, making it level. Neal scored his, then Roma scored...then it was my turn. I felt as if I were walking to the gallows as I trudged from the centre circle to the penalty area, hearing the jeers and whistles of the crowd, seeing a vast sea of photographers behind the goal, being almost blinded by their flashlights. I placed the ball on the spot, still unaware of how I would hit it. Should I blast it or try to place it in the corner? In the end I just side-footed it so slowly that the keeper could have bent down and picked it up – if he hadn't dived prematurely.

The ball rolled slowly but snugly into the back of the net. And I felt like a condemned man who had just been handed a last-second reprieve. The sense of sheer relief was overwhelming. Now, whatever happened, nobody could point the finger at me. Next man up for Roma was Bruno Conti, who had played in Italy's victorious World Cup team two years before. You would not expect him to be unnerved by anything after that. But as he walked forward to take his kick, Bruce Grobbelaar in goal performed his leg-wobbling act that was to become famous – or infamous – all over Europe. Was it gamesmanship, or just Bruce acting the clown, as he did in our dressing room – and on the pitch – so often? To this very day I don't know the answer. But it did leave poor Conti so shattered that he ballooned the ball high over the crossbar.

Alan Kennedy was our last marksman. If he scored, the trophy was ours. Some of our lads simply couldn't bear to look and turned their backs as he prepared to take the kick. But Alan was never a man to suffer from nerves. He blasted it home, to win us the greatest club competition in the world. It was a fairytale ending to a season of never-ending triumph for me. Yet within a month I was in despair.

I was over in Ireland doing a promotion for Crown Paints, our sponsors, when I had a call from Charles Roberts, who acted as my agent for a short time, to say that Napoli had been in contact with him and wanted to buy me. As I said before, I had no real ambition to leave Liverpool. But when I hurried back to Liverpool and discussed the deal with Roberts, it made my eyes water. Napoli were ready to pay me *one million pounds* just to sign on for them. I'd also earn nearly another million from a three-year contract. It was unbelievable. I would be able to look after my whole family for the rest of our lives.

There was one stumbling-block. It was Thursday – and the Italian transfer deadline for the new season was only forty-eight hours away. If I did not sign by Saturday, the deal was off. Roberts spent frantic hours trying to contact Liverpool chairman John Smith, who was spending a few days in London, watching the tennis at Wimbledon. He finally reached Smith early on the Friday morning – only for the chairman to refuse even to discuss the situation until Monday morning. That was two days after the deadline. I tried to make an appointment to see Smith myself, but he refused point-blank. He was on holiday and business could wait until he returned. I was numb with despair as the transfer broke down. Instead, officials from Napoli made a dramatic swoop to Spain to sign Diego Maradona.

I was so bitterly upset that I refused even to acknowledge the chairman for many months afterwards. If he walked into a room, I would walk out. And if we passed each other, I would turn my face away from him. Joe Fagan, who had been abroad on holiday at the time, called me into his office when he returned. I opened my heart to him, telling him that although I never wanted to leave Liverpool, the money had been just too much to ignore. 'I understand. Football is a pretty short career and you have to make the most of it while you can,' he said.

To this day I still believe that Liverpool were wrong to keep me – for financial reasons alone. Napoli were prepared to pay them £4.5 million. Even if we had won every trophy in sight for the next three years Liverpool could never have recouped that kind of money. And, ironically, when I did move to Italy three years later – to Juventus – the transfer fee was £3.2 million. So the club saw more than a million quid slip through its fingers, just as I did. They did make a killing in the transfer market that summer, though, selling Graeme Souness to Sampdoria.

As for me...within a couple of months, Napoli was just a faded dream. I had far more worrying thoughts on my mind – like having to have an operation for an injury that I feared would stop me ever being the same player again. I twisted my left knee in a pre-season friendly game in Ireland, and a hairline fracture of the cartilage was eventually diagnosed when I arrived back in Liverpool. I was more frightened about having to go into hospital than I have ever been about facing the most ruthless defenders in the world. The specialist surgeon, Richard Calver, did a brilliant job, but I was still out of action for nearly six weeks before I could play my first reserve game.

A whole lot of fears went through my mind during that spell. I was never worried that I might not be able to play again – a cartilage injury is pretty common in football. But what did concern me was whether it would affect my pace and my ability to turn sharply – both vital qualities for any striker. I would play again. But would it be the old Ian Rush? Or would I be just a shadow of my former self? When you have so much spare time on your hands, your nerves can get dangerously out of control. And it didn't help matters that, without the guidance of Souness, and with Dalglish going through a rare poor spell, the team was struggling. In fact, we slipped briefly into the bottom three of the league table, giving our critics a field day. But it was another psychological master-stroke by Fagan that turned the season round for me – and for the team.

I had played a few reserve games but, although I was still some way from full fitness, I felt that only first-team football could give me that cutting edge. So I asked Fagan if I could be substitute against Everton, hoping to get a twenty-minute run-out to ease myself back. 'Do you think you're fit enough?' he asked me. I told him I was, so he agreed to my request. But a few minutes later he came back out of his office and said, 'I don't think I'd better play you. Save yourself for next week.'

I spent the next couple of hours kicking a ball round the gym – and getting more and more annoyed at the way Fagan had changed his mind. Eventually I went back to his office to see him. 'What's happening? Why won't you play me?' I asked.

'If you're fit enough to be sub, then you're fit enough to play,' he answered.

I was starting to lose my temper. 'All right then, I'm fit enough to play,' I said, in a somewhat raised voice.

'Okay, you're playing then!' he said.

And so I was in the team from the start – exactly what he had wanted all along. It didn't have an instantly happy ending. We lost 1–0, one of the very few defeats by our old enemy in the Eighties.

But I came through with no ill-effects. And four days later I scored my first hat-trick in Europe as we beat Benfica 3–1. I scored again in a 2–0 win at Nottingham Forest the following weekend, which lifted us six places up the table. And while it took some time to get back to my best – and I was also hampered by a couple more niggling injuries – I still finished up with thirty goals, twenty-six for

Liverpool and four for Wales. And the team, after that faltering start, picked up brilliantly in the second half of the season.

Everton had led the table for virtually the whole season and we eventually ran out of games before we could close the gap on them. But we still finished second, as well as getting to the semi-final of the FA Cup, where we lost 1–0 to Manchester United. While the absence of Souness was an undeniable blow – any club in the world would miss a player of his combative skills and leadership qualities – it was still a pretty fair season by anybody's reckoning. At Liverpool, though, only a new trophy in the cabinet would spell success. And we had one chance left – in the European Cup. After the early victory over Benfica, we had been given a relatively easy passage into the final, beating Austria Vienna 5–2 on aggregate in the quarter-finals and Panathinaikos of Athens 5–0 over the two legs of the semi-final. That took us to a final against another Italian club, Juventus, at the Heysel Stadium in Brussels.

BRUSSELS: THE NIGHTMARE

Brussels, Wednesday, 29 May 1985

A night of infamy and slaughter. A night when thirty-eight people, mostly Italians, went to watch a football match. And died.

My career, indeed the history of Liverpool Football Club, has been interwoven with two of the most awful tragedies ever to afflict sport. Four years later the terrible afternoon at Hillsborough was to numb the nation. For the moment, though, let me just try to give you my account of the tragic happenings at the Heysel Stadium. I could never hope to present any kind of reason for what took place, because there can be no logical explanation for such senseless killing. All I can do is give a player's view of what occurred.

We were in good heart as we flew to Brussels. Although we had lost our League Championship, our late-season surge had left us brimful with confidence. We also knew that Juventus would be wary of having to face us, after the way we had mastered Roma just twelve months before. If we needed further inspiration it came when Joe Fagan announced a few days before the game that he was retiring at the end of the season. That came as a bit of a surprise to all of us, because we had expected him to carry on for at least another year, until his sixty-fifth birthday. Looking back, I'm not sure that Fagan ever really wanted the job. He'd been a permanent fixture among Liverpool's back-room staff for decades before he eventually took over, when he was already nearly sixty-two years old. As I have said, he was always a very emotional man, and perhaps he felt that his heart and his nerves simply could not stand the stress of another season, especially at his age.

Whatever the reason – and he never revealed it to us – we were determined to send him off into retirement with a trophy. We also had a new manager to impress, whoever he might be. While the newspapers speculated that Phil Neal was favourite for the job, the players guessed that Kenny Dalglish would get the nod before Neal. Whoever it was, though, we knew that the tried and trusted Liverpool way would continue. That was all for next season, however. Now we just wanted the European Cup for Joe.

It had been a difficult week for me, because injuries had left my place in doubt right up until the day of the game. In our last League game the previous week, Kevin Ratcliffe had caught me right on the shin when we played Everton – not the friendliest of send-offs from my captain in the Welsh team. I was unable to train all week, until the day before the game. Then, would you believe it, Dalglish hoofed a ball against my right hand – and broke a bone in my wrist. I had to have the hand heavily strapped before I could play.

The bus taking us to the stadium passed thousands of Liverpool supporters, all dressed in their red and white. They gave us a rousing reception and made us all the more determined to win the Cup, for their sakes – to give them something to crow about when they got back home and mingled with the Everton fans. It was a noisy, confident party that eventually arrived at the ground and walked outside to have a pre-match walk-about. I was surprised how decrepit the stadium looked, really old and run-down. It certainly did not seem the right arena for such a big game.

There was still more than an hour to kick-off at this time and there was almost a carnival atmosphere among the supporters. But what surprised us as we walked round the playing surface was that rival groups of fans were mingling together, our red and white and the blue of Juventus all waving side by side. There were Belgian fans jostling with them as well. There seemed to be no effort to segregate the followers of the two teams. While the mood there and then was good-humoured – they were all watching two teams of eleven-year-old Belgian youngsters play each other – it left me just faintly disturbed about what might happen once the serious action on the pitch began.

It is a sad but inevitable fact of footballing life that some supporters lose their tempers in the course of a game. All too often that can spill over into violence. And while sensible people can stand next to each other and have a difference of opinion without resorting to fighting, the blunt reality is that football has to be prepared and organized to snuff out any potential for trouble before it has the chance to break out. It struck me, at that moment, that here was a recipe for disaster. I just never anticipated how savagely my fears would be realized.

We eventually made our way back to the changing room, which was cramped and very stuffy. We opened the windows to let in some fresh air. We could hear the chanting from the two sets of supporters outside, getting noisier by the minute – then, suddenly, there was a loud bang, like something collapsing. Tracy and my father were in the crowd. My first fear was that a section of one of the stands had collapsed, so I was terrified as I dashed outside with the other players to see what had happened. Mercifully, the main stand, where they were sitting, was still there in one piece. Then we saw that a wall elsewhere in the ground had collapsed. We could see rows of injured supporters already being laid out on the ground. And we knew, instinctively, that something awful had happened.

We were quickly ushered back into the dressing room, where a few minutes before the adrenalin had been pumping furiously as we prepared for one of the biggest games of our lives. Now I was just numbed with shock. If all those people had been injured, then there must have been some who had died – I remember thinking that to myself as I just sat there. Not a word was spoken among the players. There was nothing to say. Each of us was totally alone at that moment. Then I saw Italian fans on stretchers, being carried past the window. I could see other supporters limping alongside them, I could hear the screams of those who were badly hurt, the anguish of their friends accompanying them.

For more than an hour we waited in our little changing room, as word eventually came in that dozens of fans had been killed. The estimates bordered on the hysterical – we were told by one person that 500 people had died. Then somebody else came in and said that there was only one fatality. However many it was, all I can recall is waiting there as if in a vacuum, as if this couldn't really be happening. I guess it was a state of shock. I know that the last thing in the world I wanted right there and then was to go out and play in a European Cup Final. But UEFA officials were involved in their own debate as to whether the game should go ahead.

In the end, they decided it should. I doubt if twenty-two footballers have ever been less prepared for a game. But I also believe that it was probably the right decision. It was nothing to do with who won the competition. If the match had been abandoned, I fear it could have lead to even more bloodshed among the supporters. People may say that such feelings merely capitulate to the violent minority, but the paramount objective at that time was the safety of those thousands of supporters still locked in the ground. Without a football match to distract their attention, an appalling situation might have grown even worse.

So out we trooped for a game that became the most meaningless in which I have ever taken part. Not one Liverpool player was able to play with any conviction. It was no more than a matter of going through the motions. Yet one or two of the Italians seemed ready for a vendetta, as if they were determined to take it out on us for what had happened. I remember Tardelli, an Italian international and one of Juventus' toughest defenders, elbowing me in the face. I felt that his conduct was sickening. Surely he and the rest of the Italian team were just as aware as we were of the tragedy that had unfolded.

We lost the game 1–0 to a penalty for an offence that happened way outside the box. But nobody was prepared to argue. It didn't seem to matter. All I wanted to do at the end was to see Tracy, who was waiting for me at a reception arranged before the game. It had been an awful night for her and all the other players' wives and girlfriends. For several hours we just sat around in small groups, hearing the full sickening story of what had happened. It was difficult to accept the fact that our supporters had been responsible for it.

We heard that they had charged the Juventus fans, who had fled to the wall, which had collapsed under the sheer weight of numbers. The violence had broken out in the very section where we had seen those rival pockets of supporters mixed in together. I felt sickened, disgusted, as the story unfolded. But I still refuse to condemn Liverpool supporters *en masse*. We have tens of thousands of loyal, caring fans who have followed us throughout Britain and across Europe for decades. They are not all hooligans. The vast majority are decent, law-abiding people who care passionately about football, and were as sickened as anyone by the events of that night.

There is a lunatic minority, just as there is around any big club, who look for trouble, who will go out of their way to cause mayhem. These are not football supporters, just yobs who attach themselves to clubs as a convenient vehicle to allow them to play out their violent games. I believe that over the years football has done everything it possibly can to get rid of them. There are no more terraces on Premiership grounds in England, and the stadiums are now all-seater. There seems to be little trouble inside the grounds, either. What violence there is is mainly confined to the streets outside. Must football be held responsible for that as well? To my mind, the problem lies with society. I don't profess to know the answers. But until we control the violent climate in which we live, we will continue to have trouble outside football grounds in the same way there are fights every night outside pubs and clubs.

Action had to be taken by Europe's football bosses. And they banned English clubs from competing in Europe for five years. It was a tremendous blow to the game in England, and I had to feel sorry for Everton, who had just won the League but would now be denied the challenge of competing in the European Cup. I felt sorry for the dozens of players and thousands of supporters who would not enjoy the thrill of European competition. But if such a ban meant that a life might be saved in future years, then it was impossible to argue against it. It was Bill Shankly, in one of his passionate outbursts, who once described football as 'more important than life or death'. Heysel showed the futility of those words.

Chapter 5

Kenny's Kingdom

There was a mood of depression hanging over English football in general when the 1985–6 season began. And it was even more marked over Anfield. The game was still in a state of shock after Heysel, and we knew that Liverpool would be on trial more than any other club. All we could do was roll up our sleeves and show that the club was not going to be pulled down by the actions of a minority of morons. We did it in style, too, winning the double of the League Championship and – at long last – the FA Cup. As is so often the case at Anfield, we didn't start off the campaign too well, but once we settled into our rhythm we hit a purple patch in the second half of the year.

Kenny Dalglish, as we expected, had taken over from Joe Fagan and was to operate in a dual role as player-manager. That meant taking one hell of a lot on his shoulders, but he sensibly leaned a great deal for help on the Bootroom brigade, recalling Bob Paisley from retirement to lend his wisdom and enormous experience. Fagan often popped in as well and was still very much one of the family. It was interesting that when Dalglish held his eve-of-season team meeting you could sense he was a bit uneasy in his new role – and at the change in relationship it would inevitably bring between him and the players. We called him Kenny at first, as we always had. And he never stopped us. But the message came through via our trainers Roy Evans and Ronnie Moran. 'You'll have to start calling him Boss or Gaffa, now he's the manager,' they told us. And eventually we did – unless it was on the field. Then he had to take the curses just like the rest of us. He was only our equal then. And he accepted that quite comfortably. Dalglish may be the greatest player I have ever played with, but he's no bighead. In fact, he shuns the limelight. And that attitude from the top reflects on the whole team. There was not a single player in those days who could ever be accused of conceit.

Perhaps it was players like Kenny, myself, Hansen and Grobbelaar who made most of the headlines, but we never saw it that way. From the day I stepped into the senior team it had been like that. And I feel that this ability to mix together, to battle together when the chips were down, made that team of 1985–6 the best Liverpool line-up I ever played in. While we had lost Souness, who ranks not far behind Dalglish for quality, Jan Molby, as good a passer of the ball as I have known, had joined us a year or so back. And Dalglish's first signing was a master-stroke, bringing hard-man Steve McMahon from Aston Villa.

He became one of the few players to play for both Liverpool and Everton. We had tried to buy him from Goodison Park a couple of years previously, but he had understandably opted to go to Villa instead, when Everton fans, angry at him turning 'traitor', damaged his car. But he had no such problems when he joined us from the Midlands. He became one of my closest pals, along with Molby and Whelan. We used to call ourselves The Gang, spending a lot of social time together.

But I don't think there was a single player in that team who didn't enjoy a drink at the right time. Liverpool have always had a reputation for being a pretty friendly club, as well as a pretty good one on the field. I have never worried about a few drinks interfering with my football. And the club always relied on the common sense of the players. Your behaviour when you were away from the club was always left up to you. What they would not tolerate, of course, was the merest sign that off-field behaviour was affecting someone's form. If that ever happened – and I know of one or two players to whom it did – they were out of the team. And out of the club, if they did not change their ways.

I have always operated my own rules. I enjoy a drink after games, when I reckon I've earned it. I might go out for a meal or for a couple of quiet pints in midweek, but never if we had a midweek game, which we almost always did. And certainly never on the two nights before a game. If the club were big enough to treat us all like men, it was up to us to earn that respect – that was always my belief.

Everton had led the table for much of the season, bidding to retain the title they had won the year before. But we gradually closed the gap in what was proving a sensational season for Merseyside. We finally moved ahead of them just a week before the end of the campaign, when we beat Leicester at home and they crashed at Oxford. It meant that if we won our last game at Chelsea we were the champions again. I recall Molby saying as we came off after beating Leicester, 'That's it. We've won the title now.' He wasn't counting any chickens. I knew exactly what he meant. He had the same feeling of certainty inside him that we all had that season that, provided we played at our peak, nobody could beat us. It is a very special feeling, which most players will not experience in their whole careers. But this was a very special team.

Dalglish had spent a fair part of the season on the bench, where he could wear his manager's hat and watch us in action, rather than being involved in the hurly-burly on the field. But he brought himself back as the title race went on in earnest. And he performed brilliantly when he came in. It was just as if we'd made a brand-new signing. He gave us just the lift we needed at a crucial time. And it was only fitting that he should score the goal that gave us a 1–0 victory at Chelsea – and the trophy we had 'loaned' to Goodison Park just for a year!

Such was the domestic domination of the two Mersey clubs that the FA Cup Final just had to be Everton v. Liverpool. And that's exactly how it turned out – our second meeting at Wembley in three years. And this one had added drama, making the pre-match tension almost unbearable. If we won we would join Tottenham and Arsenal as the only clubs in modern times to complete the famed double. We had it all to play for – and Everton had just as much reason for stopping us, to end our dreams as well as to salvage their own pride.

For the rest of the nation, though, the final was billed as a shoot-out – Ian Rush against Gary Lineker. Lineker had recently broken into the England team and had joined Everton from Leicester at the start of the season. He had scored a lot of goals for them in what proved to be his only year at Goodison Park, and already a number of people were acclaiming him as the new goal-king of Merseyside. I have no idea how he felt about the inevitable comparisons between us, because it's something we have never spoken about. But it didn't bother me. I felt I was in a better team.

The TV pundits had a field day discussing the strengths and emphasising the weaknesses – of the two of us. Like most players I get annoyed at former pros who can't resist pointing out our faults to the world once they get their faces on a TV screen.

My reaction is that it's easy to be critical when you're seated in the comfort of a television studio while the players are taking the flak on the field. I reckon that Alan Hansen, captain of our team at Wembley that day, is a perfect illustration. I have known 'Jocky' shout and scream at the television screen during his playing days, slaughtering the pundits. But look at him now! As one of the top commentators today, he's the first to dish out criticism. And, like Jimmy Hill and all the others, he's never wrong of course. Mind you, I do understand that they have to stimulate interest among the viewers. It's no use them just coming on the screen and mouthing a few platitudes. They wouldn't last half a series if they were not prepared to be controversial.

All the paper-talk was far from my mind that day, however. I had already played in two League Cup Finals at Wembley and had appeared there a couple of times for Wales. But an FA Cup Final – that was one of my greatest boyhood dreams coming true. What boy has not allowed his mind to wander and pictured himself walking out at Wembley on that greatest day in the footballing calendar? Since I was knee-high to a garden gnome I never missed watching the final on television. Now I was actually taking part! I could barely sleep the night before, I was so excited.

But it was Everton who took the game by the scruff of the neck in the opening half and threatened to destroy our double ambitions. They were that bit sharper in the tackle, quicker to the ball. And they deserved to go ahead before half-time – with Lineker scoring the goal. But while we were concerned at half-time, there was no sense of panic in our dressing room. We knew we could raise our game a couple of gears, while Everton, even at their best, had not managed to kill us off.

We began the second half much more positively. And then, suddenly, we were level – and I had scored! Molby, prompting brilliantly from our midfield, put me clear on the left with a perfect pass inside their full back. I had controlled my run, to make sure I was not caught offside, but my pace still took me beyond their defenders, with only the desperately advancing goalkeeper to beat. Bobby Mimms was in Everton's goal, in place of poor Neville Southall, who had broken his ankle while playing for Wales against the Republic of Ireland in Dublin a couple of months earlier. Mimms narrowed the angle as best he could, but I was able to slot it past him. Craig Johnston rushed forward and tried to help it over as it crossed the line. He even had the cheek to try and claim it! But Dalglish put him right. 'Good job you didn't touch it until it was in – you might have been offside!' he told him.

But Craig was the happiest Aussie in the world a few minutes later when he scored a legitimate goal of his own to put us ahead. By that stage though, so Lineker said later, Everton had already begun to sense that it wasn't their day. 'When Rushy scored, we knew there was nothing going for us. After all, when he scores, Liverpool never lose...' He was referring to a remarkable record I had. Since I had won my first-team place, Liverpool had never been beaten in a game in which I scored – a run that was eventually to come to an end the following season. For the moment, though, it had become a much-discussed oddity in the newspapers. And I didn't mind, because I felt it would only help to create extra uncertainty in our opponents.

We were never in any danger from the time we went ahead, but just to make certain of victory I scored my second a few minutes from time. I actually started the move, laying the ball back to one of our defenders and then sprinting forward. My abiding memory is of Peter Reid trying to keep pace with me to cover me. He just didn't have the legs and eventually he went sprawling as he caught my ankle. I could hear him screaming, 'You f...ing b...!' Not a very nice thing to say to a player he tried to sign for Sunderland ten years later!

I can remember grinning at him, then moving in to the right-hand side of the penalty area for a cross from our left. Dalglish made a brilliant decoy run to pull a defender away, and when the ball reached me I was unmarked, as I controlled it and drilled it inside the far post. Everton were floored. The FA Cup and the double were ours! No game before or after ever gave me the same feeling of unbridled ecstasy. People often ask me: If you had to choose one magical memory above all others, which one would it be? And I would have to choose this particular afternoon.

Everything about it was sheer perfection, from the greatest Liverpool side I ever played for, and possibly the greatest British side in history. And we had proved it. To add even more spice to the occasion – for a Welshman at least – we did not have a single English player in the team that started the final. Only when McMahon came on as a substitute did an English-born player take part in a game that made us the toast of English football! For the record, the Liverpool team comprised: Grobbelaar (Zimbabwe); Beglin (Republic of Ireland), Lawrenson (Republic of Ireland), Hansen (Scotland), Nicol (Scotland), Molby (Denmark), Whelan (Republic of Ireland), Dalglish (Scotland), MacDonald (Scotland), Johnston (Australia), Rush (Wales).

What a mixture – and what a multi-talented bunch they were. Bruce Grobbelaar had his eccentric moments but he was a magnificent goalkeeper, fearless and acrobatic. Poor Jim Beglin's career was to be wrecked by injury before he could fully achieve his potential. Alan Hansen and Mark Lawrenson were simply a phenomenal central defensive pairing. Neither were what you would call hard men, in the sense that they didn't believe their job was to lurch around kicking lumps out of opposing forwards. They both preferred to do their job with style and polish. They were, in fact, two of the most accomplished players in the side, both with far more all-round ability than I had. Put them anywhere near the opposition goal, mind, and they would invariably overdose on panic! As I have often said, scoring goals is as much about the ability to remain ice-cool as it is about skill.

I was especially pleased for Hansen, who was first up the steps at Wembley to collect the Cup, because Scotland had unaccountably left him out of their squad for the World Cup finals in Mexico the following month. I knew how deeply that had hurt him. Now here he was leading the double champions of England. The Scots must have been sick at that sight – and so they should have been. It was little short of criminal to leave out one of the best central defenders I have ever seen.

Stevie Nicol was always the practical joker of the dressing room – and the butt of everybody else's jokes as well. I have lost count of the number of times he had mysterious messages sending him to out-of-the-way meetings that were never really on. And I remember more than once Steve turning up at a function in his dinner jacket while the rest of the lads were casually dressed. He'd somehow been given the wrong information. Or he would turn up in jeans and T-shirt while the rest of us were in suits! But he was a great fall-guy and would always laugh, even when the joke was firmly on him. And I think he used to play to his audience – he realized how good it was for team morale.

In midfield Molby might not have been the fastest thing on two legs, but his passing ability was inch-perfect, as good as any I've ever come across. He also had perhaps the most thunderous shot I have ever seen. Proof of that came with his goal-scoring exploits that season. I scored thirty-two goals in all as an out-and-out striker. And he was second-top scorer with eighteen.

Dalglish, as I've stated before, was simply the King, while Ronnie Whelan was one of the most underrated players in the whole game. He had a marvellous engine, he could run all day, and he also had a brilliant tactical awareness. While he rarely made the headlines, he was a key player as far as we were all concerned. And Kevin MacDonald alongside him, despite having only a relatively short time at the club, was another unstinting grafter.

Craig Johnston, my partner up front, was generally given licence to roam as the fancy took him. He had an infectious enthusiasm and energy, which would always keep me going. He was also a non-stop talker throughout the game, which would often force me into lung-bursting runs just to get a break from him! But Craig also had great acceleration and a considerable amount of flair. Had he accepted offers to play for one of the four British national teams, rather than opt for Australia, I believe he would have made a big impact on the international scene. But I admire him for sticking to his principles, as I admired him for the way he dramatically turned his back on football a few years later to return to Australia to look after his young sister, who had been crippled. That says a lot for his character.

We celebrated long into the night after our triumph. But any hangover I suffered was swept away when I saw the newspapers the next morning. They were full of speculation that I was back on the wanted list of some of the top clubs in Europe. Terry Venables was allegedly wanting me to join him at Barcelona and several top Italian clubs were also named, including...Juventus. I didn't believe this particular story at first. How could that club ever possibly sign a player from Liverpool after what had happened at Heysel just a year before? Would their fans ever accept it – or would they revolt against it? I could not see how they could find it in their hearts to welcome me or anyone else from Anfield.

But when I arrived back on Merseyside I went to see Kenny Dalglish, who told me that the stories were true – and that Liverpool were prepared, reluctantly, to sell me. Because they were out of Europe, it meant that the club's financial resources would be severely drained. Selling me was the solution to their cash problems. While several clubs from the Continent had made enquiries, the two serious offers had indeed come from Barcelona and Juventus. I spoke on the telephone to Venables, who made me an offer that would guarantee me instant millionaire status – and I don't mean in pesetas!

Baby face – my first trophies. That's me, second from left in the back row (*top*), with a local five-a-side squad. And third from right in the front row (*above*) with Welsh Cup winners, Deeside Primary Schools team.

Previous page: The most familiar sight in football...Ian Rush salutes another goal.

Left: Love and marriage...
...and the family Rush. Tracy and me with our two sons, Jonathan and Daniel (*below*).
But it's a potential nightmare for defenders (*bottom*).

Right: What a polisher! Well, it is the European Cup, which Liverpool had just won back in 1984.

Above: The first farewell – and a goal to celebrate at Chelsea, in my last game for Liverpool before my move to Italy.

Right: The Latin look… me in my Juventus strip.

Left: Who says football's an easy life! Mind you, it does have its compensations when it comes to holiday time.

Above: Postcard from Italy – our home in Turin for a season.

Overleaf: We've won the Cup! Captain Rush celebrates Liverpool's Coca-Cola success at Wembley in 1995 as Sir Stanley Matthews gives his smile of approval.

Above: Hey, Robbie Fowler, that's my boot...

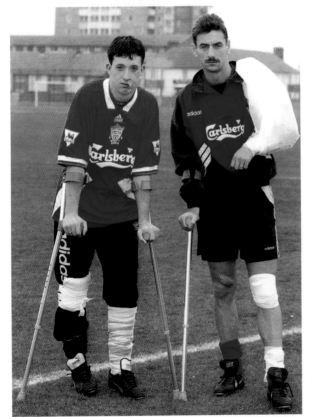

Left: And this is what happened in the argument. But it was only an April Fool's Day joke!

Previous page: A sight to strike fear in goalkeepers the world over... Ian Rush moves menacingly in for the kill.

Who says I don't get on with Italians! Luciano Pavarotti (*above*) and Frankie Dettori (*top*) both love their football.

Above: The spoils of war...me and my trophies. I had to swap the Porsche (*top*) for a family saloon though when the boys came along!

Right: Outgunning the Law man...but Denis didn't really mind me breaking his FA Cup goals record.

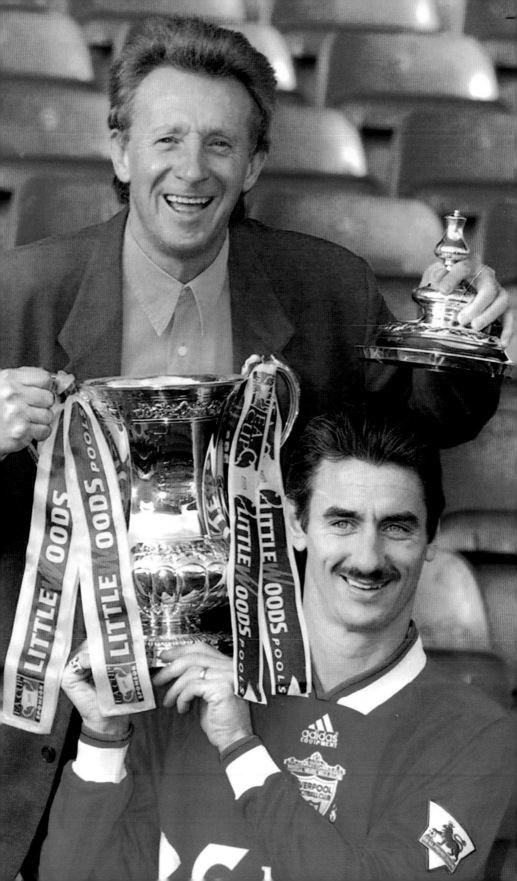

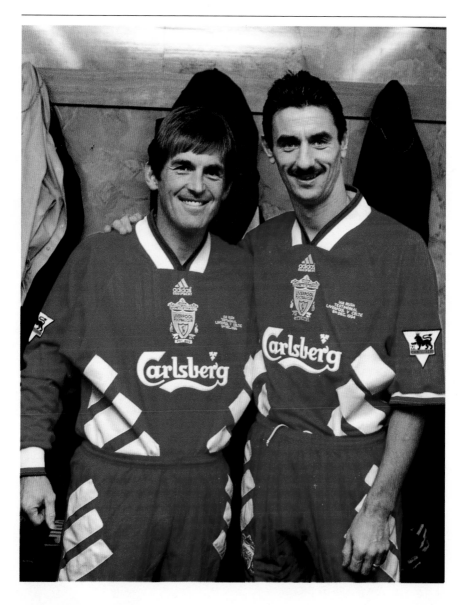

A few of the greatest...Kenny Dalglish (*above*) at my testimonial, Jan Molby (*above left*) in Japan and Ruud Gullit (*left*), shaking hands before Holland played Wales in the World Cup in 1988.

Overleaf, above: The final curtain - my last game for Liverpool at Anfield - but look who is stealing the show! Maybe son Jonathan is already launching a new Rush era.

Below: The great day at Buckingham Palace.

Mark Hughes, one of my good pals in the Welsh team, was already with Barcelona and he telephoned me several times, begging me to join him. I was sorely tempted. And Liverpool would have been paid £4.3 million for me – more than a million pounds over the £3.2 million offer they had received from Juventus. Dalglish was brilliant. 'Don't worry about the transfer fee, just go to where you feel you would enjoy your game more. And if you don't want to go at all, we'll be only too delighted to keep you,' he said. It was a tough decision for me. I loved playing for Liverpool, especially after the fantastic season we had just enjoyed.

But I knew that, financially, I had to go. I was getting married to Tracy the following summer and I had a future family to think about now. Also, because I had been at Liverpool since my teenage days, I was not one of the big earners there. It is a fact of footballing life that you get a much better deal from a club when you join them as an established player in your mid-twenties, rather than as a youngster.

After a fair few sleepless nights, I finally made up my mind to join Juventus. While their terms did not quite match Barcelona's, I would still be a millionaire. And the three-year contract would earn me nearly eight times as much as I was currently taking home at Liverpool. I plumped for Italy because I felt it was the biggest stage in the footballing world. I also think, deep down, that I wanted to try and give them something back for that tragic night in Brussels. Ironically, having failed to sign me, Venables swooped on Lineker instead.

I'm not trying to sound like a saint. If there had been a big discrepancy in the two deals, I would almost certainly have gone to Barcelona. But the situation being what it was, there was something that intrigued me about Juventus. I also regarded them as the second greatest team in Europe, second only to Liverpool. So I signed the contract, became the property of Juventus – and spent the next season, 1986–7, playing for Liverpool! The rules in Italy at that time limited foreign players to two per team. Juventus already had Dane Michael Laudrup and Frenchman Michel Platini on their books.

Platini, captain and superstar of the French team that won the European Championship in 1984, had planned to retire at the end of the 1985–6 season, but was persuaded to play for another year after his brilliance had helped Juventus to win the Italian Championship. Juventus signed me anyway, because they did not want to risk losing me. But their plan was to lend me out to Lazio, one of the two big clubs in Rome, for a season. I didn't fancy the idea, however. I felt it was a big step down for me.

Maybe, in my heart of hearts, I also couldn't bear the thought of leaving Liverpool, for all the riches that the move would bring. So I insisted that I would play another season at Anfield instead – and the two clubs agreed. What would have happened if I'd picked up a serious injury in that time, goodness only knows. Fortunately, it didn't happen. But that was certainly not because I took things easy on the pitch. In fact, it was quite the reverse. I was acutely aware that I was very much on trial that season as far as our supporters – and maybe some of my team-mates – were concerned. I had heard that when Kevin Keegan left Liverpool on a similar kind of delayed deal in the late 1970's, he had been given a tough time by the Kop. Nobody could ever accuse Keegan of not giving 110 per cent in any game he ever played in, but the fans still took his departure pretty badly. I did not want that happening to me. I felt I had had a special relationship with those supporters ever since I broke into the team, and I didn't want all that to end in acrimony. So I was determined to give them a final season to remember. I knew it was going to be a highly emotional season for me. But I was going to leave Anfield with my head held high...even if one or two of the lads had already christened me Luigi! There was only one way of achieving that – to give them as many goals as I could.

As it happened I had, from a professional and personal point of view, the most complete season of my life. I played in every single game – even in friendlies. And I scored forty goals – thirty in the First Division, six in the FA Cup and four in the League Cup. But I felt I was much more than just a goal-scorer. I ran my heart out for the team, week in and week out. I made goals for others, as well as becoming an extra defender when the other side had the ball. I believe I was maturing anyway, learning to become more of an all-round player. But I knew that nobody, absolutely nobody, could ever accuse me of having an easy ride.

The one crushing disappointment was that the team did not win a trophy – for once Liverpool's famed and feared end-of-season form let them down. We had won our last seven League games to pip Everton for the title the previous year. Now they were to have their revenge. We had a spectacular run in mid-season and were nine points clear at the top of the First Division at one stage. But then we let it slip away from us. I have never been able to understand why, because I believe we were far and away the best team in the country. Maybe a bit of complacency crept in. But we lost our way, which is not like Liverpool at all. And Everton came on strongly at the finish to cruise to the title, ending up nine points ahead of us.

We also blew a 1–0 lead in the League Cup Final at Wembley, losing 2–1 to Arsenal. That was the game that ended my long record of never being on a losing Liverpool team after I had scored. I got our goal and I thought it would be the first of a few, as we dominated the opening half. But it all drifted away from us after the break. The double blow-up at Wembley and in the League, on top of my impending departure, gave the critics a field day. They were already announcing the break-up of the greatest team in Europe.

I knew better. Dalglish didn't take very kindly to the hiccups that cost us two trophies. He was never one for a consoling arm round the shoulder and 'bad luck' when we lost. He would slaughter us in the dressing room just as angrily as Paisley or Fagan ever did. And, as I prepared to leave, I knew he would make the signings to get things right. He had already brought in John Aldridge to replace me when I left – we played together quite a few times, enough to convince me that he was a natural goal-scorer who would take over my mantle without any problems. Then Dalglish swooped for John Barnes and Peter Beardsley. The result was that the following season Liverpool would be crowned champions again. Some break-up!

But that was in the future. For now, as the current season neared its end, my mind was in turmoil. I was feeling some excitement at the prospect of moving to Italy, but was weighed down by the gut-wrenching sadness I felt at leaving Liverpool. Thankfully, our supporters were magnificent to me. I never heard the merest hint of criticism from a single one of them. In fact, I reckon they helped me through the final few games as much as my team-mates did. The title was already gone by the time we had our last home game, against Watford – but I was fiercely determined to sign off with a goal for the fans.

It wasn't much of a game, to be honest. Watford fought hard to contain us, and with seven minutes to go it was still scoreless. Then a long ball was played through their defence, I latched onto it and steered it past their goalkeeper Steve Sherwood and into the net. The Kop had been chanting my name all through the game – now they exploded in delight. And I exploded with them, as much from relief as anything. I must have scored more than a hundred goals like that one, and it was nothing special. But the moment made it so sweet.

At the final whistle the ground was still jam-packed, with everybody refusing to leave until I had given them a lap of honour. I went right the way round the pitch, all alone, the noise deafening and a vast sea of faces all around me. I could see that many of them were in tears. I couldn't believe it – why were they showing such emotion for me? Then I realized that I was crying too! I suddenly took off my shirt and tossed it into the crowd – it caused a right old scramble. And I was told that the lad who had managed to purloin it had to be given a police escort out of the ground!

There were still thousands of fans besieging Anfield an hour after the game. I wanted to go outside and give them a final salute, but the police were fearful of youngsters being hurt in a stampede. Instead I had to be smuggled out across the pitch and through another exit. I was planning to have a quiet meal with Tracy, but I was lured into a surprise party that Kenny Dalglish had organized. It was a fantastic farewell, with the whole playing squad and the back-room staff there. But, well the worse for drink, I did disgrace myself – by putting a huge cream cake over the head of Kenny's wife Marina. The boss did give me permission to do it, mind you – although he vehemently denied it to her! Marina was to get her revenge a year later, after I had returned to play in Alan Hansen's testimonial game. I had a whole gateau planted over my head!

Our last game of that season was at Chelsea, where we drew 3–3 and I marked my farewell with a goal. We went straight from London to Israel, where we had a friendly game arranged against their national team in Tel Aviv. It was to be, as I thought then, the last time I would ever pull on a Liverpool shirt. But it was a pretty embarrassing night – we regarded the trip as little more than an end-of-season jaunt and never gave it our proper concentration. We were 3–0 down before we had barely touched the ball. A half-time blast from coach Ronnie Moran brought at least a semblance of order to the second half, but we couldn't get a goal back. It was a low-key way to end it all. But really, by that stage, my mind was already beginning to drift to Italy. I was remembering, in particular, the parting words of Joe Fagan when I had gone to say goodbye to the Bootroom boys a few days earlier. 'You've had a fantastic time at Liverpool, you've loved every moment of it and you've given pleasure to a lot of people,' he told me. 'But that part of your life is over now. You've got to look forward. If you look back, you'll only make yourself miserable.'

They were virtually the very words that Alan Oakes had spoken to me seven years earlier, when I was on my way from Chester to Liverpool. I knew it was good, sound advice. I was determined to take it.

Chapter 6

The Sour Taste of la Dolce Vita

See Naples and die, that's a famous Italian proverb. Well, I have a different one: Spend a year with Juventus and die a thousand times! I think I packed a lifetime's emotions into my one season in Italy. And they aren't all bad memories, despite what the newspapers, both in Britain and in Italy, might have led you to believe. Most of my 'deaths' came courtesy of the Italian press, who wrote me off as a no-hoper every time I failed to score. When I did manage a goal, mind you, I was instantly hailed as a hero! In the end, I just took no notice. If you did, your moods would swing from ecstatic to suicidal every week.

I had already been through a long, hot summer by the time I arrived in Turin on 20 July 1987 to begin what I thought would be a three-year stint with Italy's most famous club. The trip to Israel had been followed by a break in Spain with some of the Liverpool players, a holiday in Mauritius with Tracy, a brief trip to Turin to find ourselves a home, a four-day visit to Sweden on behalf of Nike, my boot sponsors, and then – after we were married less than three weeks before our arrival in Italy – a honeymoon with Tracy on the fabulous island of Aruba in the Dutch Antilles.

My earlier trip to Turin had given me an inkling of what to expect from the most passionate football nation in the world. I was mobbed by fans at the airport, then had to answer the most amazing questions at a press conference. Would I have fought in the Falklands War if I had been called up? I could only make a wisecrack of an answer: 'I'd go anywhere for a game of football!' What did I think about the marital problems of Prince Charles and Princess Di? My answer: 'I'm not sure, really, it's been quite a while since I've spoken to them!'

They wanted my words of wisdom on Margaret Thatcher, Italian cooking, religion...even on the merits of English and Italian literature! The kinder papers had christened me The Eagle, although one or two were not so generous. One reporter reckoned that I looked 'like a cross between Adolf Hitler and Charlie Chaplin!' Well, at least Adolf couldn't sue them! Tracy took a fair bit of stick as well. She had been sitting alongside me, in front of the media, sipping a glass of Coca-Cola. By the next day the papers had revealed that she had been knocking down a few Camparis! It was quite a shock to discover that I had married a woman verging on being an alcoholic. But at least Tracy was able to give them the answers to the questions they fired at her in a smattering of Italian. I'm sorry to admit that my grasp of the language was pretty dismal at that stage.

We had both begun to learn Italian a few months earlier, but while Tracy took it all very seriously, I just kept putting it off. I had Italian cassettes, which I was supposed to play in my car, but after a few minutes I'd get bored and put some music on instead. By the time I eventually arrived in Turin to launch my career with Juventus, I realized my mistake. It meant I was going to find it very difficult to communicate with my new team-mates for the first few months, until I began to get a grasp of the language. In reality, it was far worse than I had imagined it could be.

We began with a ten-day training programme in Switzerland and I marked my début in the Juventus no. 9 shirt by scoring the first goal in our 2–0 win over Lucerne at the end of the trip. That was a relief – nearly 10,000 Juve supporters had made the four-hour journey to watch us play. But I already had a vague feeling of unease as we travelled back afterwards. I had just sat there in near-silence during the usual dressing-room banter, unable to join in because of the language barrier. And that had left me feeling lonely, very much like my first days at Liverpool. I don't have a lot of self-confidence even now, and I'm still basically shy with people I don't know.

What had bothered me more, though, was a talk I had with Michel Platini, the former idol of Juventus, who had joined us for a couple of days to keep himself fit – even though he had announced his retirement at the end of the previous season. I tried to persuade him to change his mind, to play on for at least another season. I knew what a great player he was, and I would have loved to have had him prompting me from midfield. But he said no, then he told me, 'Ian, I must tell you that you have picked the wrong time to come here. This is a bad team you are joining. And I cannot see it getting any better.'

Only two seasons earlier Platini had been voted European Footballer of the Year as he led Juventus to the Italian Championship and was an absolute inspiration to them. But it was an ageing team that had struggled last season. And even Platini, the darling of the crowd just a few months before, had come in for a lot of stick. He was not prepared to take such verbal abuse again – that's why he had announced his retirement. Juventus, never afraid to use the cheque book to buy themselves back into contention, had shelled out £10 million all told that summer, bringing in five other players as well as myself. But Platini still feared that the balance of the team would be wrong, that it lacked quality in midfield. He turned out to be a shrewd judge.

Rino Marchesi was the team manager, a pleasant, warm man and a highly respected coach, having worked at Napoli and Inter Milan. But he was in the second season of his two-year contract – and already the knives were out for him, from supporters and pressmen impatient to see the team back on top. I don't believe he had any say when it came to transfers. Most of the power at the club seemed to lie with the President, Giampiero Boniperti, once a hero himself back in the Fifties, when he played in the same team as the great John Charles, the Welshman who became a legend in Turin. The club was actually owned by one of the wealthiest and most powerful men in Italy, Gianni Agnelli, who also happened to have a controlling interest in the Fiat company, which had an annual turnover, so I was told, of nearly £18 billion. Juventus was a bit of a hobby to him – but one that he took very seriously. He attended virtually all the home games and the players would meet him every couple of weeks for a twenty-minute pep-talk at his mansion straddling Villa Perosa, the rather more humble headquarters where we used to be locked away before home games.

Agnelli was always magnificent to me, and would keep me behind after the other players had departed to give me extra advice and encouragement. While it was a real lift to have a man of his stature on my side, I often used to wonder whether it caused any resentment among my team-mates. After a few months I had picked up the language quite well – there's no better way to learn than to live in a country. But I still felt very much an outsider in our dressing room, as if there was a hostility towards me from some of the players. Some of them were great, going out of their way to make me feel at home – players like Sergio Brio and our goalkeeper Stefano Tacconi in particular. And Pasquale Bruno, a defender who had only recently joined the team from Como, became a good friend. We lived quite close to each other, so we often went out together. But others used to turn their backs on me, whisper in corners, stop talking when I came near...Perhaps I was being ultra-sensitive, but it was difficult ever to relax in that kind of atmosphere. I also suffered a hairline fracture of my right thigh muscle before the League season actually began, which kept me out of action for three weeks and took quite a while longer to heal totally. It meant that I had an indifferent first few weeks of the campaign – and first impressions count, especially in Italy. Within a couple of months, the press had written me off as a multi-lire flop. While I shrugged aside such comments, the warning of Platini was already beginning to haunt me. Juventus were not a good team in any sense. We were a collection of individuals with little pattern on the field – and little team spirit off it.

By Christmas, when footballers take a break at the half-way mark of the Italian season, we were already too far adrift of the leading teams to have any chance of winning the League. We'd also been knocked out of the UEFA Cup by Greek side Panathinaikos, which was unforgivable as far as our supporters were concerned. They had turned on Marchesi with such venom that it was pretty obvious, even by this stage, that he would be departing in the summer. I had scored just five goals so far, but the most tormenting aspect was that I'd barely had a chance created for me.

I am not a George Best or a Ryan Giggs type of player, the kind who can run with the ball to destroy defenders and make his own chances. I believe I am an ice-cold finisher, but I need players to make those openings for me. At Liverpool I had flourished on the superb work of players like Dalglish, Souness and Molby. At Juventus the harsh fact was that we did not have a single player who possessed the skills to open up defences with a telling pass. It had meant a traumatic first four or five months in Italy for me.

And I guess I took a lot of my frustrations out on my wife. Poor Tracy, who must have had her own problems adapting to Italian life, had to put up with my tantrums and moods of depression. But I thank God she was around and had the strength of character to cope with my behaviour – and bring a sense of reality back into my life. We had our rows, sure, but what married couple doesn't have occasional arguments? Some of the stories that appeared in the newspapers, however, made me furious. They alleged that I used to come home and take it out on Tracy! Over the years of marriage I've probably suffered a few verbal clips from my wife – and probably all of them have been justified! But I could never raise a hand against her. Any man who hurts a woman is not a man at all, as far as I am concerned.

While the papers slaughtered me regularly, the Juventus supporters were always brilliant towards me. I do not ever recall one unkind word from any of them. They treated me like a king. Often the youngsters would come up and touch me if they saw me in the street, just to see if I was real! When I first arrived in Turin I was a little apprehensive that they might take it out on me, as a former Liverpool player, for what had happened at Heysel just two years previously. But I honestly never heard the tragedy mentioned once by an Italian in the whole time I was there. The only people who ever talked about it were those who came over from Britain to see me.

I think the supporters took to me because I was prepared to mix with them – unlike most players in Italy, who are given superstar status and are generally very aloof from the folk who pay their wages. Pasquale Bruno and I used to call into a local open-air coffee-bar every day after training to have a drink and a bit of a chat with the locals. And they loved it. It was good therapy for me, too – the best way I knew to learn the language. I honestly felt much more at home and relaxed sitting there, sipping an espresso, than I ever did in the Juventus changing room.

But I reckon I must have spent more of my time on the telephone than training! Our phone bill while we were there averaged more than £1,000 a month. Tracy and I both called our families regularly, while I used to ring the lads at Liverpool to see how their season was developing. They obviously weren't missing me too much – they were top of the League as usual. And when I was really low, I would call Kenny Dalglish or Graeme Souness, who was manager of Rangers by that time, for advice – and, I guess, for a bit of comfort.

Maybe I shouldn't have been resorting to such measures to cheer myself up. Maybe I had left too much of my heart in Liverpool. It might have been better if I had totally turned my back on my old mates and concentrated instead on my new job. Such notions are fine in theory. But when you are as depressed and unsettled as I was, when football has stopped being fun, it's so difficult not to go back to your roots.

I had made my mind up when I returned after the Christmas break that I would be much more forceful in my dealings with Juventus – and more greedy and selfish on the field. It worked, too. I scored nine goals in the second half of the season, finishing on fourteen, a total which, in Italian football, is far from failure. I had some real highlights as well – I scored in both derby games against Torino and I had one of those magical nights in the Cup against Pescara when everything clicked. I scored four goals...and was then substituted twenty-five minutes from the end of our 6–2 win. 'You have scored too many goals already – save some for the next game,' Marchesi told me.

I had become well used to the Italian style of play by this stage, especially the tactics adopted by opposing defenders. Obstruction, shirt-tugging, sly kicks off the ball – they were a way of life over there. And, as often as not, I'd have an opponent man-marking me throughout the game. Although I had been in Europe over several seasons with Liverpool, this kind of treatment week in, week out was new and frustrating to me. But I learned eventually that patience and self-control are vital qualities over there.

There was no question, either, that it was the best League in the world, as far as quality was concerned. Most of the world's best players were there – and playing against them was a real education. The two outstanding stars of the day were Diego Maradona, who had inspired Napoli to the Championship in the previous season, and Ruud Gullit, the dreadlocked Dutchman who was making such a dramatic impact on AC Milan. Gullit was a colossus in football boots, a huge and powerful man who was also blessed with incredible skill, pace and balance for his size. He was well-nigh unstoppable when he made those surging runs into the penalty area.

He would blend into any team, anywhere in the world. For he had a genuine appetite for hard work to supplement his vast range of skills. I saw at first hand how important he was to AC Milan, as they mounted a late challenge to overhaul Napoli at the top of the table. Milan deserved to win the title. They were the best team we faced all season, they knitted together and played for each other in a way that no other side could match.

But, with no disrespect to Gullit, Maradona had to be the greatest player in the world at the time. The first thing I noticed about him, when Juventus travelled to Naples to face him, was how small he was. But he was as wide as he was tall – and his massive, muscular thighs showed just how hard he would be to knock off the ball. But his real magic lay in his unbelievable ability to run with the ball without ever having to look at it. It was as if the ball was tied to his boot laces, he was so sure of where it was. I have never known another player who possesses such a stunning quality. And it meant that he had an extra dimension to his game, a vision that no other player could match.

If you had to pick on any weakness in that magical little man, it was that he was all left foot. But what a foot! He could turn defenders both ways with it, and it was also strong enough to resist all the ferocious tackling that the Juventus defenders launched at him. You couldn't knock him down – unless he was looking for a free kick. He was adept at falling over an outstretched leg, a trick I had also been learning in Italy. Some people may call it cheating. But my view was that, like Maradona, I was being kicked black and blue by defenders, who would get away with it most of the time. So if you had the chance to turn the tables on them, you took it! Believe me, there hasn't been a striker anywhere in the world in the last twenty years who has not conned a referee into awarding him a free kick or a penalty. And in Italy, the con-trick was almost an art form!

As the season wore on into spring, Juventus continued to stutter, enjoying occasional tremendous one-off performances but never able to put a decent run together. I was quite satisfied with my own form since the break, but my private life was becoming intolerable. We had rented the top floor of a seventeenth-century mansion, high on the hillside overlooking Turin. It was an idyllic setting, with peach trees, grapevines and roses adorning the gardens. But the owner, who lived with his family on the ground floor, wanted to run our lives. He wanted me to go out with him nearly every night, meeting business associates of his.

When I began to refuse the invitations, his attitude towards me changed. He had fawned all over me in the early months, but now he was distinctly cold. And that's when stories began appearing in the newspapers about the blazing rows between Tracy and myself. I couldn't help wondering who was feeding the reporters all this rubbish. I became almost paranoid, even believing that the telephone in our apartment was bugged. It was so unpleasant that Tracy and I decided we would move out before the following season.

But would I still be with Juventus then? Speculation had already started that clubs like Liverpool, Everton and Manchester United were monitoring my situation closely. I took it all with a pinch of salt. I was beginning to understand and adapt to the Italian way of life by this time, and was quite prepared to see out the three years of my contract. But I had a nostalgic taste of the way things used to be in April 1988, when I travelled back to England to play in a testimonial match for John Charles and Bobby Collins, two of the great old-timers of Leeds United. Charles had asked Juventus if I could guest for Leeds against Everton, and I was only too delighted to oblige.

I was even happier when I heard that Michel Platini and Kenny Dalglish had both agreed to drag themselves out of retirement for this one game. I had a long chat with Charles, who had smashed Juventus' goal-scoring records by hitting more than a hundred in his five seasons with them. 'But I had my problems, too, with people wanting to run my life for me. Just be your own man, keep your head up and keep battling away,' he told me. I felt much better for that advice – and better still a few hours later when we played Everton. It was strange pulling on a Leeds shirt. How could I ever have guessed that I would be joining them eight years later? But it was wonderful to have the likes of Dalglish and Platini giving me the kind of service that I had almost forgotten during the past eight months.

Everton fielded their strongest side – and the way they tackled in the first few minutes proved that this was not destined to be just an exhibition game. It was as fierce as any League match. I found myself drifting back into midfield, just as I had been doing at Juventus, to forage for the ball – often the only way I could get it. But Dalglish yelled at me to get back up front, and I didn't need any further encouragement. It didn't take me long to appreciate him even more. We split Everton's defence wide open with a perfect one-two, which left me in the clear to slot the ball past Neville Southall. I hadn't scored a goal like that all season – and I was thrilled.

Then it was Platini's turn to take over centre-stage. He noticed me drifting wide and ordered me to get straight back in the middle. 'You don't score goals from out there!' he told me. 'You get in the area and we will make the goals for you.' He was as good as his word, too. He created my second goal with the most perfect pass I have ever had in my whole career – a chip with backspin that left Everton's defenders stranded and virtually stopped at my feet. This was just like old times! Poor Southall was left floundering again, as I sold him an outrageous dummy by pretending to shoot. As he dived desperately, I just lifted the ball over him.

No goalkeeper likes to be made to look like a mug, big Nev in particular. I knew he was angry with me. He was even madder when I completed a hat-trick early in the second half, after another superb pass from Platini had given me the chance. A few minutes later he made a brilliant save from me, sprawling across his goal to push the shot behind for a corner. As I came into the six-yard area, he looked at me and said, 'Why don't you f... off back to Italy!' I just burst out laughing. We have been colleagues in the Welsh team for as long as I can remember, but I've never asked him whether he was joking when he said that to me...

The game had been shown live on television in Italy, so I was pleased to show them that, given the right kind of service, I could score plenty of goals. It was a big confidence boost for me. But it was a bitter-sweet night in some ways. If only I had someone of Platini's class behind me at Juventus. In fact, it should have been him. He was in vintage form that evening, still good enough to be playing at the highest level. He had become a major television star instead, which obviously hadn't left him short of a bob or two. I had a lift back with him to Italy the next morning – in his private jet!

I was back in England again in May, playing this time for Liverpool against an England XI in another testimonial match, for Alan Hansen. The lads had won the League, but they had been beaten by Wimbledon in the FA Cup Final just a few days earlier, so they were a bit depressed. But the crowd soon lifted everyone – especially me. There were more than 31,000 packed into Anfield and they gave me a rousing welcome. I scored a couple of goals and we won 3–2. But if that gave me some satisfaction, my deepest feelings as I walked off the pitch were for those supporters. Even before the game I had been besieged on my way into the ground, with everybody yelling the same message at me... 'Please don't go to Everton – come back to Liverpool!' Everton had been strongly linked with me, but I knew at the end of this night that if I did come back to play in England, it would have to be for Liverpool. I wasn't quite so certain at the testimonial banquet later that night, though, when Marina Dalglish got her revenge on me – pouring a huge gateau over my head. Never tangle with a woman, especially a Scottish one!

I had to return to Italy for our final game of the season – and what a crunch meeting it was. Juventus and our arch-rivals Torino had both finished exactly level in sixth spot in the table. That was the final position for a place in the UEFA Cup the following season, so the two sides were ordered to stage a play-off for the honour. Juventus had regarded a place in Europe as their divine right – they had not missed an appearance in one of the big European competitions for more than twenty years. To fail this time would be nothing short of humiliation. It was a game we simply dared not lose.

With so much tension surrounding the match, it became a war of attrition, with neither side prepared to take the slightest gamble. A goal became about as likely as a summer snowflake and, even after extra time, there had not been even the merest hint of a chance for either team. So it all came down to a penalty shoot-out. I was nominated to take the final penalty, so I watched with growing nervousness as we missed one, then Torino missed twice. It meant that if I scored with my spot kick, victory was assured. Strangely enough, the nerves had cleared by the time I placed the ball on the penalty spot, took careful aim and stroked the ball into the net – via the inside of the post! A couple of inches wider and it would have rebounded out. Such are the tiny margins between success and failure. Not that I was too concerned about such niceties at that time. I just felt a surge of sheer relief that a season of such trials and tribulations had at least ended in a measure of triumph.

It was not enough to save the manager, however. Marchesi was told just twenty-four hours later that his contract would not be renewed. While the news was not exactly a shock – his sacking had been forecast in the newspapers ever since Christmas – I still felt a certain sympathy for him. He was a nice, compassionate man, who was never really able to exercise any genuine control over the team. That power, as I have said, lay with Boniperti, who had the ear of the owner. It was to him that I always went when I had a problem.

I still had one more game to play in Italy that season – for Wales. Terry Yorath, who had recently taken over as manager, had organized two end-of-season games, in Malta and then in Brescia, where we were playing Italy as part of their preparations for the European Championship finals that summer. With our regular skipper Kevin Ratcliffe absent through injury, Yorath made me captain for the tour, which was the fulfilment of a lifelong ambition. We had a real struggle in Valetta before beating the lively Maltese 3–2. But it was the game against Italy that really whetted my appetite.

Even before I left Turin, the Juventus players were holding up five fingers at me, the number of goals they were saying Italy would score. For some of them, it wasn't a humorous gesture either – they wanted to see Wales thrashed. And most Italians expected us to be. But while we had only our pride to play for, I was as wound up before the game as I have ever been. I had a lot of things to prove to a lot of people. The rest of the team, God bless 'em, were just as determined as their captain. The Italians, urged on by a volatile, capacity 30,000 crowd, began like wild men. Mark Hughes emerged from one tackle with his sock torn in half and studmarks covering his calf.

We got stuck in ourselves, taking them on at their own game.

And on the half-hour I managed to beat a defender to a cross and steer it in, to give us the lead. But that only served to increase the frenzy of the game, as the Italians went wild with frustration. It became an ugly, brutal war – and we were no angels! But we held on to our lead to emerge with a victory that was just about the sweetest of my whole season. Some of the Italian players were still ready for war even after the final whistle, though. I went over to shake hands with Gianini, who pushed my hand away angrily, screaming, 'You don't play fair. Wait until I see you in Roma next season...' If that was a threat, it only made me feel contempt for him. I was as bruised and battered as anyone on the field that night. But once a game is over, there is no point in continuing a vendetta.

A few days later, on 7 June, I had a long, frank meeting with Boniperti and Agnelli. I poured my heart out to them, explaining how disappointed I had been about the season just past, how I felt that the team lacked the quality, especially in midfield, to mount a serious title challenge. I also told them of the loneliness I felt in the dressing room, how I sensed animosity towards me from some of my team-mates. 'If you want me to, I am prepared to see out my contract. But I will understand if you feel you have to sell me, to bring in somebody new,' I told them.

Agnelli brushed aside such talk, insisting, 'We still have total confidence in you. We want you to stay.' He even asked me which British players I would like to have alongside me next season. I mentioned half a dozen names – Peter Beardsley, Mark Hughes, John Barnes and a few more. I felt much better and more settled for our meeting. I had always had a great deal of respect for Agnelli – I still do to this day – and within a week he proved he that was a man of instant action as Juventus made bids for both Hughes and Beardsley. Both were turned down, but I was pleased by his demonstration of faith in me.

Dino Zoff, the legendary former Juventus and Italy goalkeeper, had already been named as the new manager and that was another boost. 'He is much more positive in his attitude, he likes to play an attacking game,' Agnelli had told me. All in all, things were finally looking up as I left for the summer break. But a holiday in the Cayman Islands soon changed all that! I developed what I thought were heat lumps in the final days of the break. When we arrived back at Tracy's parents' house, where we were staying, she called the doctor – who immediately diagnosed a bout of chickenpox. I had also managed to contract a mild dose of hepatitis and shingles, as well as a liver infection.

I did not eat for a week and could barely sleep, the pain was so intense. At the end of it I looked like a skeleton, and a specialist told me that I would need a good deal of rest to build up my strength before I could even think of going back to Italy. It meant that I had to miss the beginning of pre-season training. And even though Juventus sent their own club doctor to visit me, to see just how exhausted I was, I don't think they truly believed me. When I did eventually rejoin the squad in Switzerland I was still as weak as a kitten. A brisk walk was about as much as I could muster. My first proper training session left me utterly exhausted. I began to fear, even at this stage, that I would not be fit enough in time for the new season.

The Italians had relaxed their rules during the summer regarding the import of foreign players, allowing each club to field three rather than two, as had been the case the previous year. Michael Laudrup and myself were already at the club, and when Zoff signed Portuguese midfielder Rui Barros and then brought in Russian star Zavarov, one of us had to go. Laudrup, in fact, was already resigned to leaving. Juventus had agreed terms with PSV Eindhoven for his transfer – and he was not exactly ecstatic at the prospect. It was a big step backwards, in financial terms as well as in prestige. So I was not altogether surprised when he eventually rejected the move.

But that left Juventus in an embarrassing position. Four into three just won't go. Something's got to give. I realized it could be me – but I was still stunned when Paul Dean, my advisor back in England, telephoned me on the night of 13 August to ask me, 'Would you be interested in going back to Liverpool?' I thought he was joking at first. But eventually I realized that he was being deadly serious. Liverpool, as professional as they always are, had been alerted to Juventus' problem and had moved in for me when Laudrup's transfer broke down.

Did I want to go back? Is the Pope a Catholic? I was thrilled at the prospect of pulling on that famous red shirt again. There were some regrets – I had grown really fond of the Italian people, the Juventus supporters in particular. And I knew that by moving back to Liverpool I would be accused by a lot of critics of running away from Juventus, believing that the job I had there was simply too much for me. I would have liked at least another season in Turin, just to prove to the doubters there that I could score goals. But those thoughts paled against the excitement of going back to my old club, my old mates. And it was not as if I was running away – Juventus had given Liverpool permission to speak to me, so they were obviously prepared to let me go.

In less than a week after that call I was a Liverpool player again. It all happened so fast that Tracy had to remain behind in Turin to supervise the removal of our belongings back to England. I did get a couple of days off to go back and help her, and to say my own goodbyes. The newspapers, true to form, had declared that Juventus would be better off without me! But the response from the supporters was heart-warming. Everyone I met in the street shook my hand and wished me well. I was deeply moved by them. If only I had found such friendship within the club. For I have to admit that I never truly felt part of Juventus, and never felt an affection for them. And I don't think it would have made a great deal of difference had I been there five years. I still doubt if I would have developed any real bond towards them.

Yet when I look back upon it all now, it was an experience I would not have missed. It made me rich, for a start. I was a millionaire when I returned. But, equally important, it made me grow up. I think both Tracy and I became worldly-wise in that year, living in the pressure-cooker of the world's most fanatical footballing country. We learned how to cope with a media that generally bordered on the hysterical, with the customs and lifestyle of a different country. But what I missed, more than anything else, was the banter in the dressing room. I can never remember having a good laugh.

Maybe I was still carrying too much of Liverpool inside me. Maybe I should have gone there with a swagger rather than a soft shoe-shuffle. Because the Italian media love their heroes to be larger than life. They are worshipped more than film stars over there. That's why I would say to Robbie Fowler or Ryan Giggs, or anybody else who asked me for advice: Don't be afraid of it. Go there and tell your new team-mates, tell the press, how good you are. Such posturing would not be tolerated in an English changing room, but in Italy they love it. And they believe it.

If they ask you about literature, tell them you read Shakespeare! If they ask about music, tell them that a Beethoven symphony or a Verdi opera is your kind of listening! Tell them what they want to hear – and tell them in Italian. Learn the language before you arrive – don't make my mistake. But remember most of all that Italians will always believe what they hear and what they read, rather than what they see!

Chapter 7

Hillsborough: The Grief of a Nation

I t was Thursday, 18 August 1988, when I rejoined Liverpool – just five days after the telephone call from Paul Dean. Kenny Dalglish met me at Manchester airport and drove me to Anfield for a chaotic press conference. My move had been kept such a closely guarded secret that even MI5 would have struggled to find out. So when I arrived, the whole place was in shock. The press had been briefed that Liverpool were unveiling a costly new signing. But not a single soul guessed that it was me. I was overwhelmed by it all. As soon as we drove through the gates and into Anfield, I knew I had made the right decision.

Liverpool were not the only club to make a firm offer for me. Roma had matched their bid of £3 million, while Bayern Munich were also keen on taking me to Germany. But I was told by Juventus that if I did not go to Liverpool, I would be staying in Turin. The two clubs had formed a special bond since the tragedy of Heysel. And it was only because of this close relationship that Juventus were prepared to let me go. I was pleased that my parting from them had at least been amicable – but absolutely thrilled to be back among my own folk.

'Words can't describe my feelings right now,' I told the reporters. 'This is the greatest club in Europe, in the world. They have a great squad of players. I only hope I can do my bit to keep the team as successful as it has always been.' The news of my return provoked an outbreak of 'Rush-mania' on Merseyside. The club sold 500 season tickets within twenty-four hours – a dozen times the normal daily rate. Even down in London, where Liverpool were due to begin their season against Charlton at Selhurst Park little more than a week later, ticket sales soared.

The fantastic interest made me feel warm inside, but it also worried me. People were expecting miracles, the newspapers were already speculating that I would score fifty goals, that Liverpool would win everything in sight. Such talk was foolish. They had forgotten that I was way short of fitness. My summer illness had weakened me to such a degree that I had been barely able to manage more than a token few days' pre-season training at Juventus. The rest of the Liverpool squad had been working hard for more than a month. They were playing Wimbledon in the Charity Shield in just a couple of days' time. I knew it would take weeks, probably months, before I caught up with them.

'Just judge me then, after I've had time to get myself right,' I urged everyone. I was not making excuses for myself, just attempting to cool the hysteria. But it made no difference. We're in an age of instant drama, when patience has become almost a dirty word.

I think the pressures got to me to such a degree that I came into the side from virtually the start of the season, long before I was really ready. I was desperate to play, to do well, to start scoring goals again. And I thought that match-practice was the quickest way to get myself 100 per cent fit again. But I lacked that yard of pace, that cutting edge, to such an extent that I failed to score a single goal in my first ten games. Of course I was slaughtered in the press – the British media aren't that far behind the Italians, when it comes to hysteria. And it was pointless telling them that I was only 75 per cent fit. I don't think I was ever more than that throughout that first season back.

Dalglish was a great source of comfort, however. 'Just take no notice of anything anybody else says. It's what we think at Liverpool that matters. And we all have total belief in you – the goals will start to flow again before long,' he told me. The players were just as much behind me as well, willing me to score. Even John Aldridge, who had taken over the chief striker's role while I was away, kept telling me, 'You're the greatest striker I've ever seen. There's loads more goals inside you yet.' It was nice to get such encouragement from Aldo, who must have been sickened when he kept reading that his days at Anfield were numbered now that I had returned.

He had already proved himself as prolific a goal-scorer as I had ever been. And I used to think it was nonsense when people said we couldn't play in the same team together. When we did, which turned out to be quite a lot, one or the other of us invariably scored – often we both did. In fact, John told me that only once in all the games when we were partners did neither of us score. They say the most successful strikers hunt in pairs, and maybe that's the proof of it.

It was the middle of October before I finally managed to break my duck. By that stage the more savage critics were wondering if I'd ever score again, and it was even suggested that my days at the top were strictly numbered. I never had any real fears for my career, not even at my lowest point. And I knew that eventually the goals would come again. I hadn't lost the instinct. But what used to frustrate me was that, while my mind was still sharp enough to spot the potential openings, my legs lacked the sharpness to carry me there. So that goal was a moment of sweet relief – even if it was only against Walsall in the League Cup. It wasn't anything spectacular, either – I picked up a pass with my back to goal, turned and just hit it low past their goalkeeper. 'About time' was all I could say to myself as it went in.

Peter Beardsley and John Barnes had slotted into the team since my year away, and it did not take me long to realize what gifted players they both were. Beardsley, basically a quiet lad off the field, had tremendous quicksilver skills and seemed almost to bounce round defenders. Barnes was much more of a livewire in the dressing room. I had the next place to him every day – and slaughtered him for the vivid yellow and orange jackets he used to wear. He took it well – and he could dish it out, too. It wasn't that easy for him when he first arrived, because he was the first big-name black player to play for Liverpool, and there were rumours that he would be the target for racial abuse.

I thought that was a load of old rubbish. Liverpool has been a major port for centuries, which has made it a cosmopolitan city. But he showed his sense of humour with the first words he spoke to the lads when he arrived, 'I'm here to add a bit of colour to the team!' Since then, of course, Liverpool and Everton have both signed several black players, without a word of abuse from either set of supporters. The ability of a player, rather than the colour of his skin, has been the only thing that mattered to them – exactly as it should be.

But it did not take Barnes long to show our supporters what a gifted performer he was. He proved himself to be a beautifully balanced runner, and he could glide past defenders seemingly effortlessly. He also had great vision and the ability to split defences with one telling pass. He was a tremendous striker of a dead ball – look at all the brilliant goals he's scored from free kicks over the years. But his greatest asset of all – and one that a lot of spectators have never fully appreciated – has been his sheer physical strength. When he had the ball, he could hold off two, or even three, defenders with that power. At his devastating best, Barnes was a player of true world class.

As my season continued to stutter along, Liverpool, as ever, were deeply involved in the race for the League Championship. As we came into spring it had developed into a two-horse race, with Arsenal mounting their own powerful challenge. George Graham had moulded them into a strong, efficient side, with every player giving their maximum. They were displaying a level of consistency that kept them breathing down our necks all the time. But I still believed we were the best team in England. In fact, Liverpool were on course for another double. For we had battled our way to the semi-final of the FA Cup, where we had been drawn to face Nottingham Forest – at Hillsborough.

HILLSBOROUGH: THE TRAGEDY
Hillsborough, Saturday, 15 April 1989

There are certain appalling tragedies that happen in your life that you can never forget. Yet the memories can remain so horrific that it is very difficult to talk about them. That is how I look back on that fateful afternoon now, more than seven years later. I still find it difficult to put into words my feelings on that day, when the whole world was stunned. Millions of words have been spoken and written already on the terrible events that caused the deaths of ninety-six Liverpool supporters who had the life crushed out of them.

I was still feeling my way back to fitness and was a substitute, seated on the team bench some forty yards away from the end of the ground, which was jam-packed with our supporters. Just a few minutes into the game I could hear a lot of noise coming from that end, but we had started the game pretty well and I put it down to excitement. Then, after only a few minutes more, it was obvious that there was a serious problem. Fans were beginning to spill out onto the perimeter of the pitch, then I saw police pulling down the fencing that had become a sad, but inevitable, feature of all big grounds after crowd disturbances in recent years.

The supporters poured onto the pitch in their thousands. While we had no inkling at that stage of just how great the tragedy was, we could see people being laid out, as the game was halted and we were all taken to the dressing rooms. At that moment we did not know if the game would be re-started. It was only in the hours that followed that the full horror was relayed to us. Every single player was totally numbed – and some were frightened, as they had friends and family at the game. I just sat in the dressing room until the team coach eventually departed. It was like living through a nightmare.

Only this was the second nightmare to strike at the heart of Liverpool Football Club in four years, following the Heysel disaster. Why us, why did we have to be stricken by such awful tragedy again, I was asking myself? Why did our fans, the vast majority of them wonderful, loyal fans, have to suffer like this? They were questions that it was impossible to answer because, of course, there is no answer. Nobody can ever know what fate holds in store for you every time you leave your house, cross the road, jump into a car or a bus.

Other, more relevant questions were to be raised later, as the full enormity of the tragedy sunk in. We had more supporters at the game than Forest. Should our fans have been allocated the opposite

– and larger – end of the ground? Were the police prompt enough in ripping down the fencing? Should those barriers ever have been erected on our grounds? They were questions much easier to answer with the benefit of hindsight. I can see no advantage in making anyone, or anything, the scapegoat for what happened. I am only thankful that the advent of all-seater stadiums has ensured that this kind of tragedy can never happen again.

The whole of Merseyside was plunged into mourning for weeks afterwards. Liverpool Football Club, the players, the staff, the supporters...we were all devastated. Yet such numbing tragedy can pull people together in a way that nothing else can. Perhaps it is the need to share grief. All I know is that each and every one of the Liverpool players was magnificent. We made sure that there would be a sizeable representation from the players at every funeral; we visited the families of every poor soul who had perished; we visited hospitals to comfort those who were injured; we spent hours every day just talking to people, just being there.

If such horror can ever produce a hero, that man has to be Kenny Dalglish. It is hardly an exaggeration to say that he took the grief of 50,000 people on his shoulders. He took responsibility for organizing everything the club could do to help people through the ordeal. He accepted all the pressures of the world's media, to keep it from the players. He attended virtually every sad event, after spending countless hours every day at the ground, meeting bereaved families and even having to comfort some of the players, who had become close to breaking point amid all the despair around them. How much it took out of him is something I will never know, because we have never talked about it. Nobody, not one of the players, has ever mentioned that day since.

Every year, on the anniversary of the disaster, we have held a memorial service for the victims. The families then come to Anfield to have tea and mingle with the players and staff. It is a poignant occasion, but even then the small talk is all about how Liverpool are progressing, will they win this trophy or that one. Hillsborough is never mentioned. It's not that we want to forget it. Nobody who was there will ever be able to do that, nor would they want to. But mere words seem so pointless. The fact that we are all there together is the best proof that we still care.

Even in the aftermath of such an awful tragedy, life had to go on. Football had to go on. There was intense speculation about whether the FA Cup should be continued that season, or whether it should be abandoned as a mark of respect to those who died. It was a heart-wrenching decision for the FA to have to make. Eventually, they decided that the competition should continue. Liverpool were prepared to settle for whatever decision was taken, even though football was the furthest thing from all of our minds. My feeling is that to carry on was the right choice. Of the countless supporters who had spoken to me, I would say that 90 per cent wanted to see us playing again.

It would be a sign that at least a semblance of normality was returning to Merseyside. And I felt that going on to win the Cup would be the most fitting tribute we could pay to the memory of those who had perished. By the time the replay against Nottingham Forest was arranged – this time at Manchester United's Old Trafford ground – it had become nothing short of a crusade for us. I was still on the subs' bench as we simply steam-rollered Forest to clinch our place in the final at Wembley against Everton. I couldn't help but feel a bit sorry for Forest that night. They were taking on the whole nation. The sheer intensity of the occasion simply overwhelmed them.

While we had been forced to postpone a few League games, we were still up there with Arsenal in the race for the title. We were left with a massive scramble to catch up on the fixtures, which meant that we hardly had time to blink before we were at Wembley. I was

still struggling to get fit and I knew I would not be in the starting
line-up for the final. My ambitions were already aimed at getting
myself fully fit for the next season. So I asked Dalglish if I could be
excused for the week before and after the final. I wanted to spend
two weeks at the training centre at Lilleshall instead, building up
my strength and stamina in readiness for pre-season training.

'You can't go yet. I want you on the subs' bench at Wembley,'
Dalglish told me. He explained that my goal-scoring exploits against
Everton over the years had made them fearful of me. And that, even
seated on the bench, my presence would be sufficient to make them
nervous. We also had two League games left, against West Ham and
then Arsenal the following week. Winning them both would give us
the title – and he wanted me around. So, somewhat frustrated, I had
to postpone my trip to Lilleshall for a few weeks. I sat on the bench
at Wembley and watched Aldridge fire us ahead – a lead we still
held, and looked well capable of maintaining, with just about
twenty minutes to go.

The last thing I expected in the circumstances was to be called
into action. But Dalglish told me to get stripped. He sent me on –
and pulled off Aldridge. I cannot imagine any other manager in the
game taking the step of substituting his goal-scorer. But Aldo had
run himself into the ground in our cause. It also gave me a boost in
confidence to realize that the boss still had that much belief in my
ability, even though I had done precious little to justify it since I
came back from Italy. All went well until the very last minute, when
Everton launched a final desperate attack – and Stuart McCall
snatched a dramatic equalizer.

That meant extra time. And although the lads were sick at
conceding a goal at the last gasp, I was feeling quietly confident. All
the other players had been through ninety minutes on that stamina-
sapping Wembley surface. I had barely got myself warmed up. It
meant that for the next half-hour, even though I still was not 100

per cent fit, I would be as fit as anyone else. Confidence, as I always maintain, is half the battle in football. Mine was high right now – and it was soaring into outer space a few minutes into extra time when I put us ahead, taking a pass from Steve Nicol, swivelling and then driving it low past Neville Southall.

McCall, who was having the game of his life for Everton, equalized again for them. But I felt that we were in control. I still fancied us to win. And then we were ahead again, as John Barnes sent over a perfect cross for me to stoop and head it home. We held on to our lead this time, to triumph in what must have been one of the most emotional finals that the old stadium has ever witnessed. Aldridge sprinted from the bench to hug me at the end – there was certainly no ill-feeling from him. He had scored a goal, enjoyed his part in the victory, and now he was genuinely thrilled for me.

Then Kenny walked over, put his arms around me, and just said, 'Don't tell me now you didn't want to be sub!' I was elated as I joined in the celebrations with the rest of the team, then gazed upwards at the huge sea of red and white – and Evertonian blue – around the stadium. It had been a rousing final, a game that all those supporters of both clubs would never forget. But it was more, far more, than that. It was the afternoon we brought a smile back to the faces of those supporters – and to Liverpool Football Club. If anything justified the decision to carry on with the FA Cup that season, it was the happiness of our fans at that moment.

But football has a way of kicking you in the teeth just when you least expect it. Our blow was to come within a week. We beat West Ham at home 4–0 – I played the full ninety minutes and scored, only my seventh League goal of the season. That left us with one more game to play, against Arsenal, our biggest rivals at home. We had already established what seemed like an unbeatable lead at the top of the First Division. Arsenal had to come to our ground and beat us by two clear goals to overhaul us. With hindsight, that

massive advantage probably worked against us on the night. I'm not
saying there was any complacency among the players, but there was
an unnatural caution about the way we played. Had we had to win
or draw in order to win the title, I'm sure our attitude would have
been different.

As it was, I suffered a groin strain after just twenty minutes,
which forced me to miss the rest of the game. I could only sit and
watch as Arsenal, battling to the bitter end, scored a goal to leave
the title balanced on a razor's edge. But as the minutes ticked by, it
seemed that their great challenge was in vain. We were going to
hold them. With only a couple of minutes left, I turned to Barry
Venison, who was one of our subs, and told him we ought to take
our tracksuit tops off to join the rest of the players in the celebrations after the game, when the Championship trophy would be
presented.

'I wouldn't do that, it's tempting fate,' said Venison. 'I did
exactly the same thing at Wembley just before the end of normal
time – and Everton scored. Don't tempt fate, like I did.'

I brushed aside his words. 'It won't happen twice,' I told him.
So I took off the top – it was deep into injury time by now. And
blow me if Arsenal didn't break away, for Michael Thomas to rifle
home the goal that won them the title.

'I told you what would happen!' snorted Venison in disgust.
And I couldn't blame him. I should have known better than to take
anything for granted. You would never catch me making such a
presumption again.

So the dream of a second double in four seasons was over.
Snatched from us in the dying seconds. Our dressing room was a
scene of desolation. We had wanted the title so badly, as much for
our supporters as ourselves. What was even more galling was that
we knew we were the best team in the country, for all Arsenal's
resilience. I just feel that the whole trauma of the past couple of

months had finally caught up with us. Physically and emotionally we were drained. We simply had nothing left with which to lift ourselves for that one final effort. If I felt for anyone, it was for Dalglish. He must have been washed out – and that night he looked like it.

I eventually had a week of hard labour in Lilleshall, followed by a quiet summer. And when we reported back for pre-season training for 1989–90 I felt fitter than I had done for the past two years. The shadow of Hillsborough still hung heavily over football, with all the top clubs under orders to turn their grounds into all-seater stadiums with maximum haste. Anything that improves safety must be right, but I knew I would miss those packed terraces when they disappeared, especially our own world-famous Kop. The atmosphere you got from that end of Anfield was fantastic – it always seemed worth a goal's start when we were attacking at that end.

The players just wanted to prove to the rest of the country that Liverpool, despite that last-minute heartbreak against Arsenal a few months previously, was still the best team in the land. Aston Villa, under their new manager Graham Taylor, gave us a good run for a while, but once we settled on top of the table in November we never lost our place. In fact, we had a tremendous run from that time, losing just one League game in the final five months. We were nine points clear of Villa at the end. The only disappointment came in the semi-final of the FA Cup, when we lost a thriller, 4–3 to Crystal Palace.

I think it was Barnes' finest season since I came back to the club. He was an irresistible presence, scoring some sensational goals – including a hat-trick in our 6–1 away win at Coventry in the last game of the season, to pass both me and Gary Lineker and finish as the First Division's top marksman with twenty-eight. I hit twenty-six and was well pleased with my form. I felt I had developed into a much better all-round player than I had been before my move to Italy. I was happy to make goals for others, as well as score them myself. I had learned to be a defender when the other side had possession, harrying and disrupting their defenders, not giving them time to settle on the ball and launch their attacks.

Dalglish, like Paisley before him, did not say much when things were going well. But if we suffered the odd hiccup, he would hammer us unmercifully. 'You're no use to Liverpool or yourselves unless you're prepared to give everything for this club,' he blasted us after one defeat – our first in twenty-one games! 'I'll bring in the boys to take your places if I have to.'

There never was the slightest danger of complacency setting in, and perhaps that was our strongest asset. I remember Southampton manager Chris Nicholl summing it all up perfectly, after we had overcome a 2–1 deficit to beat them 3–2 down at The Dell. 'It's the depth of know-how at Liverpool which sets them apart. Nobody else can get near them,' he said.

It was my fifth League Championship medal, the eleventh time in the past eighteen seasons that Liverpool had triumphed. No team in history has ever dominated the domestic game the way we had done over nearly two decades. It was an awesome record, which instilled fear in other clubs whenever our name was mentioned. After Bill Shankly had laid the groundwork and led the team from the Second Division to become one of the most powerful forces in the land, Bob Paisley, Joe Fagan and now Kenny Dalglish had carried the banner forward so incredibly successfully that our position seemed untouchable.

Looking back now, it's hard to believe that this was to be the last time in my years at Anfield that we would win the title which, in professional terms, counts most of all. It means that you are the best team in England. And, though it is a hard pill to swallow, the harsh reality is that Liverpool Football Club has only been among the also-rans in the 1990s. Not until that Championship pennant is hoisted over Anfield again can it claim otherwise.

The following season, 1990–1, began well enough for us. In fact, we started like storm-troopers, winning ten of our first eleven games and drawing the other one. But Arsenal, the one side we knew could match us for resilience, were never far behind. And they kept on our tails right through Christmas and into the new year. Dalglish had not been well – he had suffered an attack of shingles, which is often the result of stress. He didn't seem any different to us players but I wonder, with the benefit of hindsight, whether the emotional turmoil that followed Hillsborough, with the added pressures of keeping Liverpool at the top, had all caught up with him?

He was chopping and changing the team virtually from game to game, even after we gained victories. We reached the stage at one point where goalkeeper Bruce Grobbelaar was the only player who could feel confident of keeping his place – and that was only because Mike Hooper, his deputy, had been loaned out! We had still lost just twice in the League and were keeping our noses in front of Arsenal, when we were drawn at home to Everton in mid-February in the fifth round of the FA Cup.

The game finished goal-less, which meant a replay at Goodison Park on 20 February. It turned out to be one of the most amazing derby games ever to take place on Merseyside, finishing 4–4 after extra time – after Liverpool had led four times. Everton, give them full credit, just would not lie down and die that night. I had scored our third goal and, though we were naturally disappointed about not getting through to the quarter-finals, we were still buzzing with the excitement of the game.

Dalglish did not say much in the dressing room, though it was easy to see that he was upset at us squandering the lead four times. I doubt if that had happened to Liverpool in the past quarter of a century. There was a board meeting taking place a couple of nights later, but the players thought nothing of it. It was just routine. We went in for training as usual on the Friday morning, ready to head off afterwards to Luton, where we were playing the following afternoon. The club had called a press conference, so we knew something important was about to be announced, as the television crews and reporters turned up in their droves.

Then Dalglish, dressed in his best suit, came into the dressing room with the club chairman. We all fell suddenly silent. Then he told us, in that Scottish brogue, 'I just want to let you lads know before the rest of the world finds out – I've resigned as manager of Liverpool. I just want to wish you all the best...' He broke off at that point, tears of emotion in his eyes. I was too stunned to take the news in. I just stared blankly at him as he came across to shake my hand, as he did with all the other players. Nobody said a word. We were all shell-shocked.

Kenny Dalglish, Mr Liverpool, the greatest player the club had ever had, the most successful manager in England, had gone from Anfield. In the space of a few seconds, fifteen years of glorious achievement had just been blown away. The news hit the footballing world like a thunderbolt. Why had he gone? Rumours and speculation varied from the highly unlikely to the downright daft. He had an incurable disease...he had another job to go to...he was returning to Scotland to open up a golf club!

I took them all with a pinch of salt. Yet to this day I do not know why he quit – and I like to feel I am a good friend. It's something we have never discussed. Kenny has always been a very private person with a highly public profile. Maybe the pressures of living in a goldfish bowl finally got to him. He had given so much of his time and energy towards easing the trauma of Hillsborough, he had faced a challenge that intensified every week, trying to keep the club at the top of English football. He was the kind of man who always protected his players from the pressures of the outside world, taking them on his own shoulders. He wanted our minds to be concentrated purely on the football. He wouldn't even allow us to see the growing strain on him, in case it affected our performances. Nobody can carry such a burden for ever.

What I can assure you is that you will never find a single Liverpool player who played with Kenny, or served under him, who will ever say a bad word about him. He was held in total respect by all of us. But Dalglish's footballing achievement tells only half the story. He will always be held in affection by all of us as a wonderful, warm-hearted and compassionate human being. It's amazing to think how much I disliked him in those early months at Liverpool. I guess I learned to understand his sense of humour over the years – and to understand what he's saying, come to that!

Since he eventually went on to manage Blackburn Rovers – and take them from the new First Division to the Premiership title before moving upstairs at Ewood Park – he has become much more relaxed again, just like he was as a player. But he's still the Godfather, as far as the lads who played for him at Liverpool are concerned. I spoke to him for advice before leaving to join Leeds. And I'm sure that the likes of Jan Molby, Steve McMahon and Ronnie Whelan all had the benefit of his wisdom before they moved into management.

Footballers are resilient characters – we have to be in a life that can seesaw crazily. But I don't think we got over the shock of Dalglish's departure for weeks. You have to carry on, however. And Ronnie Moran, placed in temporary charge until a new manager was appointed, raised the battle cry even before we left Anfield for Luton. 'We'll all miss Kenny – but these things happen in life,' he said. 'The only thing that matters now is beating Luton.' We didn't, though; we lost 3–1 to a team that, with no disrespect, we would have murdered another day. That was only our third League defeat, but we went on to lose three games in a row – including that FA Cup second replay against Everton.

Arsenal nipped in front of us at the top of the table as we faltered – and they stayed there, beating us by a clear seven points at the end. It certainly wasn't Moran's fault. He did the best he could, but to be honest Arsenal had been threatening to sneak past us, whoever was in charge. We never quite fired on all cylinders after that roaring start to the season, although perhaps it was the shock of Dalglish's departure that caused our late dip in form as we lost half a dozen League games after he went. Speculation was rife as to who the new manager would be, with John Toshack emerging as the front runner. It made sense – Liverpool going back for one of their own. But when the new boss arrived, just a couple of weeks before the end of the season, it was another of our old boys – Graeme Souness.

Chapter 8

Souness – and the Wind of Change

I was thrilled when Graeme Souness became our new manager. I believed that if anyone had the right qualities to keep Liverpool at the top, he was the man. He was an inspirational captain when I first broke into the team, and he was as hard and ruthless on the field as any player I had ever known. He had also stamped himself as a great future manager. In my early days at Anfield I felt that he had more of the attributes in that direction than Dalglish. He was a born leader of men, with the strength of character to make players listen to and respect him. And he had the charisma to handle the directors and the media.

Most important of all, he had been brought up the Liverpool way since he had joined them from Middlesbrough. He knew how the club operated, the magic formula that had kept it at the summit of British football for so many years. He had also proved himself a bold, brave and incredibly successful manager with Rangers, where he had built up a team that was dominating the Scottish League. He took a massive gamble when he moved up to Glasgow, by spending big money to bring in English players. The likes of England players

Chris Woods, Trevor Steven, Butch Wilkins, Mark Hateley and a whole bus-load more had trodden the tartan trail to Ibrox.

There was a lot of native suspicion at first from the Rangers fans. If the Anglos had not produced the goods, Souness would have been slaughtered. But it turned out to be a triumphant move and he became the uncrowned king of Glasgow. So determined was Souness to make his own impact up there that he even tried to sign me when I left Juventus. What that would have made their supporters think, I do not know – because I am a Catholic. And Rangers, at that stage, had never had a Catholic on their books.

But Souness was the kind of man who detested bigotry, of any kind. I think that was part of the reason he wanted me. When I joined Liverpool instead, he broke the religious taboo by signing another Catholic, Mo Johnston – from arch-rivals Celtic! This, then, was the stature of the man charged with the task of maintaining our position as the most powerful club in the land. It was seven years since he had left us, and some of the younger players did not know him personally. 'Don't worry – he'll be perfect,' I told them. 'He's just the right man for the job.' Sadly, my words were to be proven totally wrong. It just did not work out for Souness. And it has to be said that he brought at least some of the problems on himself. He ripped up the tried and trusted formula that had produced so much success since Shankly's era and tried to run the club his own way. And he tried to do too much.

Souness' first season in charge, 1991–2, was an important one for Liverpool, because we had finally been allowed back into Europe after being banned for six seasons after Heysel. We were in the UEFA Cup and determined to do well. Dean Saunders, my striking partner with Wales, and England centre half Mark Wright had both been bought in the summer, and I thought we had a squad well capable of challenging for honours again. But the very first day of pre-season training showed that things were going to be drastically different. We were running longer and harder than we ever had before at such an early stage.

We had just had our summer break, and I don't believe that the limbs and muscles of the players had been hardened sufficiently for such strenuous work. It produced an incredible series of injuries to the lads, before a single ball had even been kicked – and I suffered as badly as anyone. I was on crutches within weeks, after damaging the Achilles tendon in my left leg. I was in plaster for a month, missed virtually all the pre-season training, and it was deep into the season before I was able to play. Barry Venison and Jimmy Carter suffered identical injuries, and we seemed to have half the squad in trouble with one problem or another. If we had trained in the summer before reporting back – the way we had to at Leeds – it might have been different.

Souness himself was still a superbly fit and rock-hard character. He never made us do anything that he did not perform himself – he was always among the front runners on those long runs. And because he could manage them without too much discomfort, he could not understand why everyone else could not match him. The problem is that people differ, and some have a lower threshold of pain and injury than others. I don't think he could ever accept that. With our injury toll almost reaching epidemic proportions, perhaps he was forced to rush players back into action too soon after they had recovered.

Those players on the road to recovery had to train harder than anyone else – we were ordered back for extra training in the afternoons. I could understand his thinking – to a degree. But gruelling hard work is not always the answer. In some cases it may be, but other injuries will be aggravated by too much stress, too soon. I don't know whether there was any connection with the injuries I suffered that season, but within a month or so of returning I was out again, needing a cartilage operation. And I had to undergo a second one in January 1992, after breaking down yet again. We had already been knocked out of the UEFA Cup by Genoa at that stage, and a season that had held such promise was already proving a real let-down for me. It was also the final year of my contract – and I began to wonder whether it was going to be my last season at Anfield.

The season was into its last month before I began to feel anything like fully fit. Manchester United and Leeds were battling it out for the title, while we were down in sixth place. We had no chance of getting involved. But we had managed to scrape through to the semi-final of the FA Cup. We had not exactly set the world on fire by doing so – victories over Crewe, Bristol Rovers and Ipswich had taken us to the quarter-final, where we edged home 1–0 against Aston Villa. Our luck held in the semi-final when we drew with another club from outside the Premiership, Portsmouth. It was vital to capture at least one trophy, because this was also Liverpool's centenary season, and we did not want it just to pass into oblivion.

You could tell by this stage that the pressures were getting to Souness. The strain showed in his face. And he must have suffered agonies at Highbury, watching from the sidelines as Portsmouth threatened to blow our season apart. The game was goal-less after ninety minutes, then Darren Anderton gave Portsmouth a shock lead in extra time. There were just two minutes left when Ronnie Whelan, whose goals always seemed to be so precious, scrambled in an equalizer after John Barnes' shot had hit the post. We were saved. But we were shocked when we went back to the dressing room and Souness told us that he was going into hospital the next morning to undergo a triple heart by-pass operation.

The news stunned us and our supporters, but the newspaper picture of him after the operation was altogether too much for our fans, because it was published on 15 April – the third anniversary of the Hillsborough disaster. I'm sure that Souness never intended any kind of insult. But from then on his relationship with many of the fans was never quite the same. I don't believe he ever recovered from that error, as far as they were concerned. He was still in hospital, and Ronnie Moran was back in temporary charge for the replay with Portsmouth at Villa Park. It was another grim war of attrition, which did not produce a goal. In the end it came down to a penalty shoot-out. And Pompey finally blew it, missing three of their first four attempts. Barnes, Saunders and I slotted ours away to put us through to the final, against yet another non-Premiership team, Sunderland. We certainly could not complain about our luck. It must have acted as a tonic to Souness as well. He had watched the game on television. And he vowed, 'I'll be at Wembley as long as the doctors say it's all right – and maybe even if they don't!'

I still had no idea at this stage whether I was going to be offered a new contract by the club. I was beginning to play at my best and was only sorry that the season was not just starting, rather than nearing its end. But we did have two crucial games as our finale – the FA Cup Final, which came just six days after our last League game of the season, a home fixture with my bogey club, Manchester United. I had never scored against them, in twenty-three games of trying. And it had become a bit of a national joke. The papers built the record up every time we played them. Even Tracy used to have a chuckle!

To make this occasion all the more exciting, United and Leeds both had a chance of winning the title on the very last day. Leeds were just one point ahead. So there was never the remotest danger of us taking the game lightly, even though Wembley was so close. Our old rivalry with United would never allow that. I had scored only three League goals all season – those injuries had limited my appearances to little more than a dozen. But I had a feeling inside me that my luck would finally change this day – strikers are a strange, superstitious breed; we get almost a premonition of when things are going to go well. And it took just eleven minutes to end that decade of famine. Barnes and Molby carved the opening for me to rifle the ball home.

It was lucky the goal came so quickly – I had to hobble off ten minutes later with a kick on the knee! But we really clobbered them that day, and Mark Walters scored a second near the end to complete the victory that ensured Leeds would win the title. The knee injury was not a problem, but the incredible injury list that had dogged us all season carried on right to the final. Both Barnes and Whelan were ruled out, although Graeme Souness had recovered sufficiently from his operation to be at Wembley for the Cup Final. He kept away from all the build-up, letting Moran continue to take control.

This was my third FA Cup Final in six years, and it was strange, looking round the dressing room before kick-off, to realize that only Bruce Grobbelaar, Steve Nicol and Jan Molby had survived with me from that first victory over Everton, back in 1986. Rob Jones and Steve McManaman, two of our most promising youngsters, had forced their way into the side, Wright was our new captain – and Michael Thomas, whose goal for Arsenal had cost us the Championship just two years before, was now in our midfield. The ghosts of that previous side, of Hansen and Lawrenson, of Dalglish and Johnston, came flashing back to me for a moment. Football is a game, a life, that is for ever changing. How that struck home with me in those few minutes.

It would be difficult to compare the Liverpool team created by Souness to those great sides of the Eighties, because injuries meant that we were barely able to play at full strength all season. But at least we rode our luck in the FA Cup to end the season in relative triumph, defeating Sunderland 2–0. Those wonderful North-East fans did not stop cheering for their team right up to the final whistle, but I felt that their triumph lay in just getting to Wembley. Although the match was goal-less at half-time, we were never in serious trouble. Michael Thomas put us ahead within a couple of minutes of the restart, then combined with Dean Saunders to make a second goal for me.

It was my fifth goal in an FA Cup Final – a record, and one of which I remain proud to this very day. No player could ever become blasé about playing and scoring at Wembley. And the FA Cup is something else again. The eyes of the whole world are on you that particular afternoon. It was specially significant for me, because I had still not been offered a new contract. For all I knew, it might have been the last goal I would ever score for Liverpool. But my form towards the end of the season had been good enough for the club to decide that I still had a future with them. They offered me a three-year deal, which I was delighted to accept. 'I want to see out my career at Liverpool. I can never really imagine myself playing for anybody else,' I said publicly. And at the time I believed it.

Within a few months, though, I was beginning to believe once again that my future might have to lie away from Anfield. Although we had won the Cup, I felt that the team was not ticking over properly. The mounting injury toll did not help either, causing changes, almost from game to game. It meant a very unsettled team that did not really get the chance to blend together. And that led to poor form on the field. Souness was back in control, still with a huge appetite for work – but perhaps just wanting to do too much. I could understand his feelings, for he was trying to do things the way he had done at Rangers – and nobody could dispute his amazing success there. But for a man who had been seriously ill, it was a daunting schedule. He also had to contend with supporters who were still bitter about that controversial photograph of him. And as our performance dipped alarmingly and we slipped into the bottom half of the table, he was the man who took the blame – to such an extent that speculation began to mount about his future.

I was having a miserable time up front. I didn't feel I was playing badly, but I just wasn't getting the right service. Chances were coming about as frequently as tidal waves in the desert. Bolton dumped us out of the FA Cup; Crystal Palace knocked us out of the League Cup; and by February we were looking in real danger of sliding into the relegation dog-fight. It was an unthinkable situation for a club like Liverpool. And Souness' growing desperation produced a thunderbolt for me – when I was dropped from the team for an away game with Sheffield Wednesday.

I had never been left out, apart from injury, since I established a regular place in the team eleven years before. I was shocked and deeply hurt. And it was certainly not just a case of a bruised ego. If I had been playing badly, I would have accepted the situation. If I had been missing chances, I would not have been doing my job properly – and would have deserved to be punished. But I wasn't scoring goals because I wasn't getting a semblance of decent service. That's why I was angry – and why I began to wonder where my future lay.

I sat in frustration on the subs' bench for that game, and again for the next match, at home to Manchester United. I was called into action in the second half and responded by scoring one of the best goals I've ever hit – a thunderous volley. We still went on to lose the game 2–1 to a side that would go on to win the Championship. And defeat sent us tumbling to sixteenth in the table, a dire position for a club that, until the previous season, had not finished out of the top two in a decade.

But that goal got the old instinct burning inside me again. And I decided that the only remedy, the only way I could make my point to Souness, was to become as selfish as I had ever been in my younger days. Since then I had learned the value of playing for the team, of looking for a colleague better placed than me, rather than purely shooting on sight. But now I changed all that. I became blinkered in my thinking. Goals were all that mattered. If I carried on scoring Souness could not dare even think of dropping me again. It may have been a selfish philosophy – but it paid off. I scored the winner in our next game, against Queens Park Rangers, to lift us a few places up the table. And I carried on scoring, right through the last couple of months of the season. I ended up scoring eleven goals in our last thirteen games. And Liverpool climbed to sixth place in the table, making light of all those earlier worries.

The local paper, the *Liverpool Echo*, voted me Player of the Season on the strength of those last couple of months. And, just as the previous year, I was simply wishing that the season could carry on, because I had hit such a rich vein. Despite what had happened, I had not fallen out with Souness in any big way. But there was an edge between us. And it was Souness who patched it up, by calling me into his office and telling me that he was making me captain for the new season 1993–4. Frankly, the thought of being given such an honour had never dawned on me. But I was thrilled to accept the job. I knew I had matured considerably over the past half-dozen years – especially in my season in Italy. Well, I was thirty-one years old by then!

Seriously, I had already begun by this stage to look towards the future, even to the point when my playing career was over. I had decided that I did have the qualities to make a good manager – an idea that would have made me laugh a few years before. I recall in my early days at Liverpool, when scoring goals and having a good time were my only two concerns, Phil Neal, our captain at the time, told me, 'You'll never make a manager. You don't think enough about the game.' I think it was Neal's way of trying to make me grow up a bit. He was right in what he said. I didn't have a serious thought in my head about the game.

That's not unique, it's a stage that most young players go through, until they are eventually confronted by reality and the need to look beyond their own little world. I've seen Robbie Fowler go through the same barrier. I've watched him grow from a cheeky kid who thought his goals were all that mattered into a player who now plays first for his team. Maybe he'll be a Liverpool captain one day! For me at this point, however, I had a big season coming up – my testimonial year.

Fowler was just breaking into the first team at this stage and the pair of us began well enough. I hit my first domestic hat-trick for three years against Ipswich in the League Cup – the Coca-Cola Cup, as it had become by now. And while I wasn't scoring too many in the League, I was helping Robbie to bang in plenty. In fact, he had a go at those who were criticizing my own lack of goals, saying, 'Rushy always has two defenders marking him tight, because other teams are frightened of him. That gives me the time and space I certainly wouldn't get without him around.' But that did not stop the manager from dropping me in November 1993, for the second time in less than a year – I was left out once again, ironically, against Sheffield Wednesday at Hillsborough.

I was really hurt, but Souness assured me that I was still club captain and it was only a temporary measure. And I was brought straight back into the side. But if that left me resentful, I was downright livid the following month, when I was pulled off eight minutes from time in our away game against Sheffield United. If I had been having a nightmare game, I would have accepted it. But I knew there were other Liverpool players out there at Bramall Lane who were having a far worse time than me. I was so angry I ignored Souness in the dug-out and went and stood at the entrance to the players' tunnel to watch the remainder of the game.

Had another club dangled a contract before me right then and there, I was so bitter that I think I would have signed it. Even though it was my testimonial year – I had a big game arranged against Celtic at the end of the season – I was prepared to walk out, if this was the way I was going to be treated from now on. I went to see Souness and laid my cards on the table. 'I have never wanted to leave this club, but if you don't want me, then I'm ready to go,' I told him.

'Forget it. Your future is here,' he answered.

I was not to know it then, but it was Souness who would be leaving Anfield – within a month. The crowd had been growing increasingly frosty towards him. Although a lot of our troubles were caused by injury, they did not like the way he was constantly chopping and changing the team – evolution, rather than revolution, had always been the name of the game at Liverpool. And they were especially angry when he sold Peter Beardsley to our neighbours Everton. They had come to enjoy his darting style. And when he began so brightly for the team just across Stanley Park, it did not make things any easier.

Once again the Championship was way out of sight – we were only fifth in the table, having to look on as Blackburn Rovers and Manchester United battled it out. And the final straw for Souness came when we were knocked out of the Coca-Cola Cup by Bristol City, before our own disbelieving fans. He resigned three days later, on 28 January. Despite the speculation that he was forced to go, the truth is that David Moores, the Chairman, and Peter Robinson, the Chief Executive, both urged Souness to change his mind and stay – at least until the end of the season. But he was adamant. Souness is a proud man, a winner. The fact that his team were out of contention for the honours for a second successive season was too much for him to take. And perhaps that lack of success was affecting his health.

It had been a torrid final two seasons for Graeme and for Liverpool. And a lot of the supporters were not sorry to see him go. But I felt a genuine sadness for him, despite our differences. I still held a lot of respect for him – and I liked him, too. From the time I had broken into the senior team he had been around, to drive me on, to build up my confidence, yet make sure my feet always stayed firmly on the ground. He was a huge, larger-than-life character, who knew how to enjoy himself as well as how to put his heart and soul into the game.

And although he was a hard man as a manager, he was nothing like the kind of image that people presented of him. We had some good times while he was in charge. He used to like to take players away for an afternoon's horse-racing or golf, and liked nothing more than to see his whole squad happy and relaxed, enjoying themselves. If he had been able to build on the success in his first season, when we won the FA Cup, he would have been a brilliant boss to play for. But it just didn't work out for him.

Chapter 9

Back in the Old Routine

There really was only one man to take over as manager when Graeme Souness left us – Roy Evans. He, along with the likes of Ronnie Moran and Tom Saunders, had been at the heart of the club throughout my years there – and even before that. That famed Bootroom was really the engine room of the club. It was where all the planning was carried out and the team decisions made. Evans had been a vital part of that team ever since a serious injury had forced him to retire as a player when he was still very young. He had looked after the kids, moved up to take charge of the reserve team, then graduated to first-team coach, along with Moran.

He knew the club inside-out. He was popular and well respected by the players – and, importantly, by the fans. He brought in Doug Livermore, a Scouser through and through, from Tottenham to take his place on the coaching team and that delighted me. I had known Doug for many years, since he was coach to the Welsh team under Mike England's reign, and I had a lot of time for him. Evans also told me that I would remain team captain, after I had assured him that I wanted to stay at Liverpool, despite those offers he told me he had received from Leeds and Manchester City.

While the club was not exactly in turmoil when he took over, it had gone through a transitional spell in the previous two or three years. Now we were back on a stable footing again. With nothing left to play for in the three months remaining of the season, the new manager used the time to prepare his plans for the following year. We slipped back a bit in the League to finish eighth – our lowest position for more than twenty years. But the important thing was that, by the end of the season, a cluster of our younger players, such as Steve McManaman, Robbie Fowler, David James and quite a few others, had built up experience that would be invaluable to them in the future.

Perhaps the kids had been thrown into the deep end of Premiership football a little too early, but now they were hardened, with up to fifty games apiece behind them. That's why I felt a good deal of confidence when we launched ourselves into the 1994–5 season. I knew we had the nucleus of a side that was ready to challenge for honours again. We had a good blend of youth and experience. And we certainly kicked off in brilliant style, winning 6–1 away to Crystal Palace, who had just been promoted. We played some superb football that afternoon. The result made the whole country sit up and take notice that Liverpool were back on the old glory trail. The critics, as ever, had been quick to write us off. This was the perfect answer.

As captain, I was genuinely excited at the blossoming talent emerging around me. There was a bit of a generation gap between me and quite a few of the players, but I never felt like the old man. If I had been struggling to keep up with them in training, then maybe I would have done. But I was still as fit as any of them. And having them around helped to keep me young. The only time I really noticed the difference was when we were travelling on the coach to away games. Somebody always brings a music tape to play and I had got used to the sounds of the Eighties. Now I was having to listen to new groups like Oasis, sounds I would never have heard, if it wasn't for the kids. I guess they kept me in tune with the music of the day!

I never felt any kind of envy towards the younger players because of their age. I was just happy, as captain, to try to help them progress, the way the older pros had looked after me when I was still young. I was particularly pleased to see young Fowler really beginning to blossom, scoring plenty of goals and showing a lot more to his game as well. He would often come and ask me for advice – and what I liked was that he would actually act on what I told him. It gave me a great deal of pleasure to see something that I suggested to him actually come off.

As the season wore on, though, we just lacked that hard, steely edge to mount a serious challenge for the League title. On our day we were breathtaking, and we would murder teams. There was not a more exhilarating sight in football than Liverpool in full flow. But perhaps we put too much energy and effort into those games. Maybe some of the youngsters got a bit carried away, thinking we could turn on the same style every week. The hallmark of a truly successful team is to be able to battle it out for 1–0 wins on days when you're ankle-deep in mud, days when you're not quite on top form. It is the kind of asset a team will gain only through experience – and this particular Liverpool team was still learning the art.

We were never far away from the leaders, but we were never able to mount one of those long, consistent runs to enable us quite to catch up with them, either. Mind you, I believe that our supporters understood the situation, and they still packed into Anfield for every home game. And they loved the style of the team.

Those fans also paid me a moving personal tribute that I will never forget, just before Christmas in 1994, when nearly 30,000 of them defied the pouring rain to give me a rousing salute for my testimonial match against Celtic.

I'm generally a fairly unflappable, relaxed type in the dressing room, not normally the kind who suffers much in the way of nerves before a game, but that night I suffered more tension than I can ever recall. I wanted the whole occasion to be successful, but even more than that I desperately wanted to repay everybody who turned up by playing well – and scoring a goal. I had asked Kenny Dalglish, who was now forty-three years old, if he would like to come along and play in the veterans' game we'd organized before the main event. 'Are you being cheeky – I want to play in the proper game!' he told me.

He was a distinguished Celtic old boy and I think he wanted to show the Scots that he still had some magic left inside him. I warned Robbie Fowler beforehand, 'If you think I moan at you on the pitch, just wait until Kenny's behind you!' In the event, Dalglish showed some vintage flashes as we pulverized poor Celtic. But I just couldn't get in on the scoring. Then, with only about ten minutes left – we were already five goals up – Dalglish's shot was beaten out by Packy Bonner in the Celtic goal and it dropped for me to tap it home. The crowd roared, even the Celtic fans who had been chanting my name all night just as loudly as the Liverpool supporters. For me it was just a feeling of sheer relief. I hadn't finished up looking like a mug!

I did not score too many that season – just a dozen all told in the League. That did not bother me too much, because I knew I was playing reasonably well, helping to make goals for others, especially Fowler, who was knocking them in from everywhere. But what did begin to concern me was that I might make my mark as the only Liverpool captain in the past quarter of a century not to lift a trophy.

I did not know how much longer I would be in the job, so I desperately wanted to see the team win something that season.

I knew we lacked the consistency to win the League title, so the two knockout cups seemed the best bet. We were the kind of team who could win a cup, anyway, if we turned on our best for half a dozen games. We reached the quarter-finals of the FA Cup, only to be knocked out 1–0 by Tottenham – a last-minute goal from Klinsmann plunging Anfield into despair. I had scored one of the goals in our 2–0 win at Wimbledon in the previous round, my forty-first in the competition all told – equalling the all-time record of Denis Law. Our manager Roy Evans went overboard that night, declaring publicly, 'Ian Rush is the greatest goal-scorer there has been in British football.' I didn't feel that way as we trudged off after the defeat by Spurs. But there was one avenue still open to us – the Coca-Cola Cup.

I did not score in the second round, as we cruised past Burnley. But I hit both goals when we beat Stoke City 2–1 in the next round, to take us into the last sixteen. The draw was not exactly kind to us – we were paired away to League champions Blackburn, managed by my old mate Dalglish. But we really clicked that night, taking Ewood Park by storm as we cantered to a 3–1 victory – and I got a hat trick, my last for Liverpool, as things turned out. I had not scored in our previous nine games and I was well aware of whispers from outside Anfield that my days there were numbered. You'll always get that kind of campaign orchestrated against you once you're over thirty.

It was also my six-hundredth game for Liverpool, which made the goals all the more special. And the first one, which set us on our way to victory, ranks in my top half-dozen – a left-footer I caught perfectly, to send it flashing past the helpless Tim Flowers. Dalglish was man enough to come over and shake my hand when he saw me later, although we didn't talk much. But what he told the press really made me proud. 'I've got the England centre forward, Alan Shearer, in my dressing room. And I've just told him how much he can still learn from Rush,' he said.

We had another mountain to climb in the quarter-finals, in the shape of Arsenal. But at least we were given home advantage this time. Like so many previous games between the two sides, it was an unrelenting battle to break down their cast-iron defence. But we finally achieved the breakthrough on the hour. And I got the goal again, tucking the ball away after John Barnes and Neil Ruddock had carved out the opening with a free-kick routine we had practised on the training ground that very morning. That took the number of my goals in the competition to forty-seven, just two behind the all-time record held for donkey's years by Geoff Hurst.

Who can ever explain why, but the League Cup under its various names has always proved a lucky competition for me. And for Liverpool. We were drawn to face struggling Crystal Palace in the semi-final over two legs. But they made us battle all the way, holding us to a 1–0 deficit at Anfield before we went down to Selhurst Park and beat them there by an identical score. Fowler was the hero this time, scoring both times. But I wouldn't have cared if they had been scored by the tea-lady. Liverpool were back at Wembley for the first time in three years. And this was my golden chance to lift a trophy – and be able to hold my head high alongside the likes of Phil Neal, Phil Thompson, Graeme Souness, Alan Hansen and Ronnie Whelan, who had all experienced that euphoria of triumph during their times as captain.

I had been to Wembley often enough – in fact, one of our supporters who kept a season-by-season record told me it would be my seventeenth visit to those famous Twin Towers. When I worked it out, I had been there four times before in the League Cup, three times for FA Cup Finals, seven times in the Charity Shield and twice for Wales against England, before the British Championship was sadly abandoned. In my younger days I was there so often that it became almost a regular pre-season and end-of-season date in my diary.

But the majority of the team had never been there before. This was our first final of any kind for three seasons – too long for a club of Liverpool's stature. The Nineties had been a pretty barren time for us, after all the incredible successes of the previous decade. And the critics, never loath to put the boot in, had already dismissed the club as a spent force. This was our chance to show the world that Liverpool were back, ready to challenge to regain their place at the summit of English football.

No matter how many times you've been through it all before, you never lose the thrill of playing at the home of English football. I was just as excited as any of our youngsters as we spent the week preparing for the final, and then travelled down to London to face Bolton Wanderers. Although Bolton were a division below us, I certainly did not take them for granted – or allow any of the other players to have even the slightest hint of complacency. I knew they would be tough opposition. They were pushing strongly for promotion and, indeed, went back to Wembley at the end of the season to secure their Premiership place by defeating Reading in the play-off final. I rated their management team of Bruce Rioch and Colin Todd very highly as well. They were both distinguished players and I knew their team would be well organized and coached.

When you're young, the whole day of the final flashes before you so quickly that you hardly have time to draw breath, let alone savour the occasion, before it's gone. I was determined to enjoy every minute this time – I was aware that it might be my last major event. And I did enjoy it. I loved watching our supporters, cheering us on in their thousands as the coach taking us to the stadium passed them en route...I loved feeling the atmosphere build up as we walked out onto the pitch to test the conditions, then that growing excitement in the dressing room as kick-off time approached...Most of all, I enjoyed leading the team out along that long tunnel into the sudden daylight, to a full-throated roar from the fans of both teams. No amount of money, nothing in the world, can ever buy you that kind of feeling.

Bolton, as I had expected, were full of enthusiasm and energy. And they had some moments of their own before we eventually got into top gear and began to control the game. But what we did have at Wembley that day, to really lift us above Bolton, was a display of individual brilliance from Steve McManaman. He just took over the show, running Bolton ragged with his intricate dribbling skills, carving their defence wide open time and again. McManaman had already established himself as a regular in the Liverpool side over the past few seasons, even though he was still a youngster. Ever since he first surged into the team, his skills and flair had been outstanding. Our supporters had already grown to love him for the way he would always be willing to take on defenders and, more often than not, leave them floundering. But he was a winger in the true sense of the word. There were times when he would become mesmerized by his own skills – and he would forget that football is about passing the ball as well as running with it. Fowler and I would run into goal-scoring positions, waiting for the pass that never came. Then you would want to throttle him. But five minutes later he would weave his way past a trail of defenders and score a brilliant goal. Then you would forgive him for his earlier forget-fulness – and be grateful that you had a player of his genius on your side.

Off the field, McManaman is a very sensible kind of lad, clever enough to look after himself quite well. He's also one of those natural athletes – I would back him against anyone in the Liverpool dressing room in a race over 100 yards, or 1,000. And he runs with an easy, effortless grace that makes it all the more galling for lads who have to sweat and strain to keep up with him. However, we did manage to grab him both times when he scored two superb goals to win the Cup!

By a strange coincidence, it was Sir Stanley Matthews, revered by those old enough to have seen him play as the greatest English winger of all time, who made the presentations after the game. Climbing up those thirty-nine steps to the Royal Box, with people applauding and slapping you on the back, was another highlight. And taking the Cup from Sir Stanley and then turning to hoist it aloft, for thousands of supporters to celebrate, was spine-tingling. Someone asked me later if I was ever frightened of dropping the trophy. 'No way – I wanted to be able to get my hands on it so badly that I never wanted to let it go!' I answered. It was back in the dressing room, after our lap of honour, that I was finally able to sit down and enjoy that inner satisfaction that comes from achieving something you have set your heart on.

We ended the season by finishing fourth in the Premiership, which I felt was a reasonable achievement for what was, in the main, such a young team. My contract was up in the summer, when I became a free agent. I did not want to leave – at that stage I still hoped to end my playing career at Anfield. And when Roy Evans offered me an extra year's contract, I accepted it. I would have preferred a two-year deal, but I could understand his position. I was thirty-three years old then and there were questions in everybody's minds as to how much longer I could continue.

Everybody's bar mine, that was. I knew I still had the enthusiasm – and the legs – to motor on for a few more years. Even when Stan Collymore was signed from Nottingham Forest for £8.5 million, I still felt capable of keeping my place in the team. If I had not suffered that cartilage injury, who knows what might have happened during the past season? But if strikers are supposed to be dreamers, I am a realist as well. I leave Liverpool with one major disappointment – that I was not quite able to surpass Roger Hunt as the club's top all-time League goal-scorer.

But I was able to establish one notable record in the last few months. I came on as a substitute in Liverpool's 6–0 FA Cup romp over Rochdale on 6 January – and scored the goal that finally passed Law's record tally of forty-one. I had set my heart on that target for a long time, because the FA Cup is the most romantic competition of them all. So I was thrilled. And Law took it pretty well. 'I've been proud of this record. It's stood for more than twenty years and it's kept my name alive in the minds of people who did not even see me play,' he said. 'But if it had to be broken, it had to be done by a player who has been outstanding. Ian Rush has been that – and more. He has been the best goal-scorer since Jimmy Greaves. He's the only one, in my eyes, who has been up there with the great man over the last thirty years. And he's done it year in, year out for so long.'

I wouldn't mind a tribute like that on my tombstone...

Chapter 10

Dream Team

D on't live in the past...that is a message I have drummed into myself and into others for just about my entire footballing life. Yet when it comes to naming my all-time Liverpool XI during the fifteen years that I played for them, the fact is that not one of the present team wins a place. Indeed, the entire team comes from the Eighties, a decade when the club were the cream of Europe, perhaps the best in the whole world. I certainly do not intend this as any kind of slight on the players I have just left. There is enormous potential among the current squad. Players like Robbie Fowler, Steve McManaman, Jamie Redknap, David James and quite a few others have glowing careers ahead of them.

But I do not believe these players have reached their prime yet. They can get better. I have plumped for players whom I saw at their absolute peak. One or two of them have had to be moved slightly away from their best positions, simply because they were too good to be left out. A few others were left out purely because I can't name more than eleven players! It was very difficult to leave out a man with the sublime gifts of John Barnes, for example. But I feel that his greatest season, when he was flying down the wings before being moved into a more midfield role, came when I was away in Italy.

Craig Johnston, our madcap Aussie, was another who came desperately close to selection. His pace and appetite for hard work were a vital part of our success when he was in the side. Phil Thompson was a great combination of hard man and cultured defender. Little Sammy Lee was another who worked like a beaver for the cause. They would all be among my substitutes, ready to make their mark if any player in the team showed the slightest sign of falling below the standards they set. But the team I have chosen, in 4–4–2 formation is: Bruce Grobbelaar; Phil Neal, Alan Hansen, Mark Lawrenson, Steve Nicol; Steve McMahon, Graeme Souness, Jan Molby, Ronnie Whelan; Kenny Dalglish and myself. As any Liverpool supporters old enough to be shaving will tell you, that is a team to strike terror in the hearts of anyone having to face them.

Bruce Grobbelaar often used to win games for us by his very presence in the dressing room. He was such a comedian that he could cure all the nerves and tension that inevitably build up before a big game. He was just as much an extrovert on the pitch, a larger-than-life character who was loved by our fans. He was totally fearless, prepared to throw himself in where the boots were flying. And, like all great goalkeepers, he liked to dominate his area. That's why he would come out to the edge of the penalty area – and sometimes beyond! – to take those crosses.

If he missed one or two in the course of a season, that was accepted by us, because Bruce was a man whose acrobatics and brilliance would save us far more often. In any case, he built up a marvellous understanding with his defenders, who would automat-ically drop back to cover the goal-line when he charged forward. There was a time when I rated Grobbelaar and Neville Southall, my Welsh colleague, the best two goalkeepers in the world. And if Nev got the nod as the very best, it was only because he was just a little bit more consistent than Bruce.

Phil Neal was already an established English international, at the veteran stage of his career when I first came into the Liverpool team. He was a really cultured player, who loved to come up and support the attack – and scored some vital goals for us. He had a great understanding with Sammy Lee, who would drop back to cover him when he made his runs. He also had a wise old head – he would readily hand out advice to younger players like myself, without you ever feeling he was trying to impose himself on you. He was also ice-cool enough to be our penalty-taker.

Alan Hansen and Mark Lawrenson have to be bracketed together, because that's what they were – a brilliant team-within-a-team at the heart of our defence. I cannot imagine any other team in history having a better or more reliable combination than these two. They were also perfect for Liverpool because both were blessed with tremendous skills. Neither would ever waste a ball when they won it; they would always look for a red shirt to pass it to. Our hallmark has always been the passing game, and their ability meant that we could always build from the back. Hansen played alongside Phil Thompson when I got into the team, and Thompson himself was such a good player that when Bob Paisley signed Lawrenson he tried to devise a system whereby all three could play at the back together. It was the first time an English team had attempted such a tactic and it did not really work out.

Lawrenson was the more mobile of the pair. Indeed, he played in midfield for us more than once. He was never what you'd call a hard man, although he could look after himself. But it was the timing of his tackles that was so brilliantly effective – he made it look quite effortless. He also scored some vital goals for us. Goal-scoring was Hansen's one major blind spot. Put him anywhere near the opposition penalty area and he'd immediately start to suffer from a nose-bleed! He's the only player in the team, in fact, who would not get you a goal or two when you needed it. But I would willingly put up with that. His rock-solid defensive skills and his ability to ping a perfect forty-yard pass more than made up for it.

Jocky, as Hansen was known throughout Merseyside, had a bit of a temper to go with his Mr Cool image. He also had a dry sense of humour, and was for ever taking the mickey out of everyone. Lawrenson wasn't shy, either. I used to get changed between the two of them for several seasons and the banter used to keep me in stitches. I remember Mark causing a sensation when he came back for one pre-season with his hair dyed blond! He took some right stick for that. A lot of players have copied him since – just look at Gazza. But Mark was, I think, the first. He must have thought he needed it, in order to stand out among the rest!

Steve Nicol could have won a place anywhere. He's probably the most versatile player in the whole team. I'm not really sure where his best position was...maybe it was right back, where he often played. Perhaps it was in the centre of defence. He could even help us out, when injuries brought problems, in midfield. I've picked him at left back simply because I had to find a place for him somewhere. It means that Alan Kennedy, a real Geordie battler, had to be left out, which was a difficult decision to make because he was a smashing, whole-hearted player.

But Nicol was a superb performer, and had real pace and power as well as flair. He was also a regular goal-scorer – I reckon he could have made it as a striker if he ever put his mind to it. And he had an enormous enthusiasm for the game. I have known him play with injuries that would have ruled out many a lesser character. Like Grobbelaar, with whom he used to share a room on away trips, he was also invaluable for the morale of the team, because he became the butt of so much humour. We used to wind him up without mercy and I never once saw him lose his temper. I think that a lot of the time he would go along with the joke because he knew the value of a good laugh in the dressing room. You can't show more devotion to the cause than that!

Steve McMahon, who would be playing on the right of midfield, is another player selected away from his best position, which would be more in the centre. But, like Nicol, he was a player who was simply too good to be left out. I don't think I have ever known a more honest, willing or brave performer than Steve – ironically, the only true-blue Scouser in the team. Of course he actually was a true-blue early in his career, playing for Everton. But our fans came to respect and admire him from the very first tackle they saw him launch himself into. That was one of literally thousands that he made on the team's behalf.

At times he was actually a little bit too honest for his own good. He would get stuck into crunching tackles when he did not really need to. It meant that he got hurt too often for his own well-being. He could also be a trifle impetuous, and would get drawn into trench warfare by the opposition. But that was the manner of the man – he always wore his heart on his sleeve. That's why his ankles and shins were black and blue when he hobbled his way back to the dressing room. The scars of war they were – as often as not he'd have blood pouring from cuts and gashes to his face as well. But when the heat of battle was raging all around you, he'd always be the man at your shoulder, always there ready to help you out.

Graeme Souness was very much in the same mould as McMahon – only more so. I watched Graeme dive fearlessly into tackles that would make me wince – and I was on his side! He really was a hard man, as tough and ruthless as they come, a if he was carved out of Scottish granite. But while his ferocious combative approach labelled him a dirty player in some quarters, I never thought that. A dirty player is someone who hits you from the back, from the side, when you are off your guard. Souness never performed like that. He went in from the front, boot against boot. He was hurt himself – more often than you would ever know to look at him. But he just defied pain, and he would never let the opposition see if he had been injured.

I don't recall ever being involved in a 50–50 challenge with him on international duty, when Wales played Scotland. I was always too fast for him to get near me! But what made Souness such a special player were his qualities of leadership. There are half a dozen or more possible captains in my side, but I would have no hesitation in giving the honour to Graeme – the finest skipper I ever played with. In my younger days especially, he never allowed me to ease off the throttle even if we were winning 3–0 and I had already scored a couple. He would sidle over to me and tell me, 'Come on, you're losing your concentration. I want another goal from you.' He would really keep me on my toes.

He also found time for a laugh and a joke on the field, when the occasion permitted. But you were never allowed to smile for too long before the deadly serious stuff began again. And if I was having a rough time from any particular defender, if I'd been flattened a couple of times, he became my minder. He would walk up to the culprit and warn him in no uncertain terms, 'Do that to Rushy again and you'll have me to contend with next time.' Invariably, those few quiet words – and the menace in them – would be sufficient!

He would also lift my spirits. 'That guy's only kicking you because you're so much better than him,' he would tell me. Words that did the world of good to a young player still feeling his way in the harsh world of big-time football. He was a leader off the pitch as well, and would willingly help to sort out our little personal problems and was a perfect buffer between the team and the management. I just could not imagine a better all-round leader than Graeme – the fact that he was a fantastic footballer on top of all his other attributes made him an absolute inspiration.

Jan Molby might as well have taken his armchair to sit on when he went out to play football – he never seemed to move more than a few yards from his midfield spot for the whole ninety minutes. And the game was a stroll, rather than a helter-skelter ride, for our great Dane. But when he had the ball, he was an education to every youngster watching from the sidelines – quite simply, he was the most perfect passer of that ball I have ever known. People talk about Jurgen Klinsmann and Peter Schmeichel as the best foreign imports into our game over recent years. But I believe Molby had a bigger impact even than those two great players.

For ten years he was a lynch-pin in that midfield, and nearly everything flowed through him. He settled in so quickly after he joined us that he was an instant hit. And he loved playing for Liverpool – in fact he loves Merseyside so much that I reckon he will eventually settle there, rather than return to his native Denmark. He's a Scouser by inclination, if not by birthright! He was a hard man, too, when the need arose – like every man-jack in this team, he could look after himself. He also possessed a real block-buster of a shot – probably the hardest striker of a ball in my team.

If pace was somewhat lacking in his make-up, well, he never needed it – as he used to tell us himself. 'Just give me the ball – and I'll guarantee it goes to a red shirt,' he would say. And invariably he would live up to his boast. He was a brave man, too. I remember him playing virtually the whole of the second half of one game with a hamstring injury, because we had already used up our allocation of substitutes. Despite the pain, he was still able to ping those forty-yard passes with unerring accuracy – and with either foot. We had our laughs about him in training. I would take out a piece of turf, about a yard square, for him to stand on during the five-a-side games! He'd stand on it as well, hardly ever moving off it! 'I don't need to,' he would say, after he still made more telling passes than anyone else.

Ronnie Whelan's selection might raise a few eyebrows from the uninformed. But he was one of the first names on my team-sheet – and anyone who has played in the same team as the slim Irishman would instantly agree with me. Whelan was the ultimate players' player – only when he was absent through injury did we fully appreciate how invaluable he was. There was nothing flash or fancy about the way he played. His role was well defined: get the ball and give it to Molby or Souness, the play-makers. But winning possession, though it was hardly a glamorous job, was equally vital to the side – perhaps even more so. Without the ball, the best players in the world are hamstrung.

Whelan can be a terrier in the tackle, and could disrupt the opposition by getting among them. But he was also a very brainy player, a thinking footballer. He could read the game brilliantly and that would enable him to cut out more balls from the other side than any other Liverpool player I have known. His ability to spot situations almost before they were happening would enable him to turn a good pass from them into a bad one. He was also an unselfish and willing runner off the ball when we had possession – he must have made countless openings for me by dragging defenders away from goal, giving me those few yards of space and time that were so vital.

Kenny Dalglish was, in a nutshell, the best of the lot. He was as close as you will ever come to the perfect player. You will already have seen his name mentioned often enough in this book to show my feelings about him. I just count myself very fortunate – and privileged – to have had him as my partner when I broke into the team. They say that the best strikers come in pairs. And we hit it off as a twosome right from the start. Dalglish, though he was not jet-paced, had all the attributes of greatness – close-quarter skills to round defenders, a powerful shot, that ability to make time and space for himself...and, most of all, tremendous awareness and vision.

We developed this telepathic understanding between us. If I made a run across goal and Kenny had the ball, I did not even have to look up to see what he was doing – I knew a perfect pass would be delivered towards me, so precise that I would not even have to break stride to take it. He was not a prolific goal-scorer himself, by that stage of his career, but much of the reason for that lay in his total unselfishness. If Dalglish had the ball, with an 80 per cent chance of scoring, and I was in a position where I had a 90 per cent chance, he would give the ball to me. Personal glory meant little to him – he was the ultimate team-player. As long as we won, that was the only statistic that mattered in his book.

There is no question that I learned more from Kenny than any other player. I have tried to put as much as I can into my own game, especially now that I'm getting older and, I hope, a bit wiser. Maybe I don't score as many goals as I used to, but I like to think I have helped others in the way Dalglish helped me. With Robbie Fowler, for example, I used to play the ball into space, rather than to his feet, because I knew he had the pace to get past defenders – just the way Kenny would play it to me.

So there we are – that is the dream team I would have around me. A combination of power and skill that would be just about unbeatable. Every man-jack of them was a hard, abrasive talent, and there was not one who would ever shirk a tackle, yet each was also a truly gifted player. And, perhaps most important of all, they were all winners by nature. You would only have to count up their medals to discover that. In a perfect world, of course, I could also name the opponents. And three centre halves I would never choose to play against are Paul McGrath, David O'Leary and Tony Adams. I have suffered enough from that trio already!

McGrath, especially in his days with Manchester United, was a brilliant defender. He was hard and raw-boned, but always scrupulously fair. And he had real pace. I could never find a way round the massive frame of O'Leary, either. He was very mobile for a big man, with those great long legs that would stretch out to scoop the ball from you. And as soon as he went, Arsenal replaced him with another great defender in Adams. Tony has had his critics. He was cruelly labelled a donkey by some. But, as I'm sure George Graham, his manager during most of the glory years at Highbury, would confirm, Adams was the crucial figure in their success. And it's the same with England. It's when Adams is ruled out through injury that you realize what an integral part of the team he is, both for club and country. He may not be the most naturally gifted player around, but the key to his success is that he plays to his strengths. He is a firm, dogged tackler, a great leader of his back line – and a great captain, who will drive himself forward to get his fair share of goals as well.

As I have already said, Neville Southall was the finest goalkeeper I ever came up against – even though I always seemed to have the knack of scoring against him. And as far as strikers go, England had a lot to thank Gary Lineker for – he had a wonderful international record. Mark Hughes, my colleague for years in the Welsh team, possesses a remarkable combination of athleticism and sheer brute strength, which has made him feared throughout Europe. But Alan Shearer is my idea of a perfect centre forward.

England are fortunate indeed to have such a wealth of good strikers right now – Les Ferdinand, Robbie Fowler, Teddy Sheringham and Ian Wright will score you a bundle of goals – but Shearer has to be the best of the lot. He has everything needed for the job: power, pace, courage, a rocket shot and strength in the air. He is also a selfless worker and will run all day for you. He is just as prepared to make goals for others as to score them himself. And, on those dreaded off-days from which all strikers suffer, when chances are missed and nothing goes right, he will never let his head drop. He keeps plugging away, knowing that only hard work will change his luck. Quite honestly, I just cannot spot a weakness in his game.

While Fowler operates more by stealth than by muscle, I see similar assets in his game as his career develops. He is learning that graft is just as vital a part of his game as craft. He will get better and better, as long as he maintains his appetite – I think he is England's outstanding striker-prospect. But Wales have their own ace for the future in Ryan Giggs, whose unbelievable talents are now really beginning to flourish at Manchester United. His potential is so awesome that it's frightening.

Chapter 11

Dragon's Fire

I was once asked if I ever wished I had been born an Englishman. I won't repeat my answer – it was more or less unprintable! Well, it was one hell of a question to ask a proud Welshman. But I knew what he meant. Playing in a major final, either the World Cup or the European Championship, is an ambition of mine that is sadly unfulfilled after sixteen years in a Welsh shirt. And what makes it all the more galling is that Wales so often came so heart-breakingly close to gaining that place in the sun. If I had been wearing that white shirt of England, perhaps I would have had my moments on those great stages. But I tell you something – if I had been English, my international career might have been over almost before it had started.

I gained my first cap back in 1980, just weeks after my move from Chester to Liverpool. In fact, I pulled on the red shirt of Wales before I had worn Liverpool's red shirt. I came on as a substitute against Scotland at Hampden Park in the British Championships, which were so sadly ended four years later. I did not make much of an impact as we lost 1–0. And I struggled on in the same vein for the next two years. It was not until May 1982, in my eighth international, that I finally broke my duck, scoring twice in a 3–0 thumping of Northern Ireland at Wrexham.

Mike England, the manager at the time and later to become a good personal friend, had spotted enough potential in me to keep me in his plans, even though I took time to adapt to the totally different demands of international football. 'Rushy has that spark that will make him one of Wales' greatest players one day,' he said. Even though he has been gone from the scene for nearly nine years now, I like to feel I justified Mike's faith in me. I have scored twenty-eight goals for Wales, breaking the record of Ivor Allchurch as the country's leading goal-scorer.

But the point I want to make is that, had I been English, I very much doubt if I would have been allowed the luxury of seven games without a goal. The pressures from the media on the national side are so great that the newspaper headlines would have been screaming that I was a failure after one game. After three or four games, the demands on the manager to leave me out would have been overwhelming – and it would have taken a brave man indeed to ignore them. I am not exaggerating in the slightest. I have seen it happen to English players, strikers in particular, time and again. The demands for instant success, so often made by people who do not have a clue about professional football, are nothing short of hysterical.

I need only cite the example of Robbie Fowler to prove the point. Robbie, although he has done remarkably well for Liverpool, is still very much in the learning stage of his career – especially at international level. Terry Venables, the England manager, introduced him sensibly and gradually into his squad over the past season, giving him a couple of outings as a substitute and then a full game. Not unnaturally, Fowler, though he showed plenty of promise, did not score. But it did teach him an invaluable lesson in just how accomplished defenders are at the very top level.

However, on the strength of just ninety minutes, barely a blink in a player's career, he was instantly dismissed by some critics as falling short of international quality.

It was a ludicrous judgement. Fowler will be so much the wiser – and better – for his blooding. But those foolish criticisms will have done nothing to help him. Fortunately, Robbie's a typical Scouser and will let most of it simply wash over him. But there have been players whose careers at club level suffered because of the welter of scorn poured on them while playing for England. That's why I urge those critics who condemn without thinking to be a bit more fair-minded. Constructive criticism does no harm when it's needed. But a smattering of common sense from the press-box would do wonders for the morale of the England team.

Even as a Welshman, I have to admit that a successful England team is important for the domestic game. It creates a general interest, which will encourage more kids to want to play and more adults to want to go and watch. I still believe the FA were selfish, though, in abolishing the British Championship back in 1984. They were well aware how important the tournament was financially to the likes of Wales and Northern Ireland – and they seemed to forget how many players from those two little countries had graced the Football League over the years.

Perhaps they were a bit nervous of being embarrassed by their country cousins – after all, Wales had beaten England twice and drawn once in the last five games between the two countries! I certainly never felt inferior to any Englishman when I pulled on that Welsh shirt. In my years in the team we have produced a cluster of world-class players. The likes of Neville Southall, Kevin Ratcliffe, Mark Hughes and Ryan Giggs would have walked into any international team, anywhere on Earth. Players like Dean Saunders, Peter Nicholas, Terry Yorath, Mickey Thomas, Joey Jones and Brian Flynn have been a valiant supporting cast, all of them outstanding for

Wales over the years, and each one of them ready to sweat blood for their country.

The eternal problem for a small country like Wales, with limited numbers of top-flight professional players, has invariably been in getting the balance right. We might field a side with a decent attack and midfield, but with problems in defence. Then, when the defence was right, we might be lacking something in midfield or up front. They are the three parts to football's jigsaw. And though it might appear quite simple to fit them together, believe me it's been the downfall of countless managers ever since the game was invented.

I have served under five managers in my time with Wales. Poor Mike England failed by a fingertip to qualify for two World Cups and two European Championships before he was cruelly dismissed in 1988. I will never forget his last game in charge – because the aftermath produced a situation as close to mutiny as anything I have ever known in football. It was in the November of 1987 that we went to Prague to face Czechoslovakia in the last game of our European Championship group, knowing that victory would take us through to the finals. If we failed, Denmark would win the group.

The Czechs were already out of contention, and such was the lack of interest from their supporters that the stadium was virtually deserted. But we shrugged off the eerie lack of atmosphere to batter them for the whole of the first half. I was playing in Italy with Juventus that season and was some way from full fitness. I missed a couple of good chances. If either had gone in, I am certain it would have set us up for a convincing triumph. But the Czechs, thankful for the let-off, came back to score in their first real attack right on half-time – a blockbuster from fully thirty-five yards.

For all our possession in the second half we could not summon an equalizer – and the Czechs broke away again a few minutes from the end to score a second time. We were out – and our players, already broken-hearted, heard in the dressing room that England was the man being blamed by the FA of Wales and that he was facing the sack. Sorrow turned to blind rage among the players. England had done just about everything right in his preparations – we had let him down, myself in particular, on the field. Why should a man we respected and liked be made the scapegoat? The senior players held an impromptu meeting at Prague airport while we were waiting for our plane to take us back that same evening – and we vowed that if our manager was sacked we would go on strike and refuse to play for Wales again. We also made sure that the councillors from the FA of Wales who were with us on the trip were fully aware of our threat.

I think it stunned the people who ran the game in Wales. It took them another three or four months before they eventually decided not to renew England's contract, after a lot of bitter argument among the FA of Wales members, a number of whom wanted him to remain in charge. It was Mike himself who, when he got to hear of our threat, persuaded us to take a more rational view. And by the time he was ousted, a lot of the heat had gone out of the argument. By that point he may even have felt a touch of relief to be leaving, believing that a change of manager might produce a change of luck for the team. Mike certainly has not suffered since – he opened a couple of residential homes in North Wales and nowadays spends much of his life playing golf. I even hear he scored his first hole-in-one recently!

His departure paved the way for Terry Yorath to take over. And what a baptism he had. Our qualifying group for the 1990 World Cup finals included Holland and West Germany – the two best sides in Europe! We never had a chance, and we had a pretty dismal time of things, even losing to Finland. It was a difficult situation for Yorath, who had played with the senior players in his squad and now had to become their boss. I think it took him a year or so to settle – and it was Peter Shreeves, his coach, who helped him so much. Shreeves, once manager of Tottenham, knew the minds of players inside-out. As well as being an astute tactical coach, he was also the kind of man who loved a laugh and a joke with the lads. I think he helped Terry to relax. And after his settling-in period Yorath became a fine manager.

We were desperately unlucky not to qualify for the 1992 European Championship finals. We drew the mighty Germans – again! – in our group, but beat them at Cardiff Arms Park when I scored the only goal. We also took three points out of four from Belgium, which was a great achievement – but the Germans went one better, taking all four points from the Belgians, to pip us to top place in the group by a single point.

If that was sickening, the 1994 World Cup produced the biggest night of despair of all. We had begun our qualifying group games with a disastrous 5–1 mauling by Romania in Bucharest, but had clawed our way back so well, in a group that also included Belgium and Czechoslovakia, that we had only to win our last game, at home to the Romanians, to book our passage to the finals in America. They were a good side, no question about that, and dominated the first half to take a 1–0 lead. But we scrambled an equalizer through Dean Saunders early in the second half – and suddenly there was total panic in their team.

Within minutes we had been awarded a penalty. Had it gone in, I am convinced that the Romanians would have crumbled totally and we would have emerged handsome winners. But poor Paul Bodin saw his kick rebound from the crossbar. You could almost see the relief flooding through the Romanian players, who took over again to beat us 3–1 in the end. My eyes were moist as I trudged from Cardiff Arms Park that evening. I felt that my last chance of appearing in the biggest competition of them all had gone. But I was just as gutted for those wonderful Welsh supporters, who were still chanting for us, despite their own heartbreak. For their sake alone, I would have loved to see the country finally triumph.

Once again it was the manager who emerged as the fall-guy – Terry Yorath was sacked a couple of months later. But what more could he have done to get us to the USA? If that penalty kick had been six inches lower, Yorath would have been the hero of Wales. Now he was the victim of our latest failure. His dismissal also blew wide open the sense of togetherness he had so carefully cultivated. The fans were in uproar – so much so that they chanted Yorath's name when John Toshack came over from Spain to take control for one game. Toshack was so disturbed by it all that he quit after that one night in charge.

Mike Smith, once a reasonably successful Welsh manager back in the Seventies, was recalled to try and restore some stability to the scene. But, nice man though he was, Smith had been away from the professional game for a long time. The qualifying campaign for the 1996 European Championships was a disaster, as we crashed to stunning defeats by the likes of Moldova and Georgia, let alone Bulgaria and Germany, our eternal rivals. Smith was gone before the end of the campaign...and it caused some raised eyebrows when my name was linked with the job. I never actually applied for it because I still wanted to carry on playing for at least a few more years. And I wasn't sure I could give sufficient concentration to the two jobs. But that did not stop the speculation from continuing in the newspapers for weeks. Neville Southall actually applied for the job, being prepared to manage the team on top of his goalkeeping duties. And I know that there was quite a considerable volume of support for me, certainly from the fans. In the end, the FA of Wales decided it would be too much of a gamble to give the post to an untried, untested manager. But I make no secret of my ambition that it is a job I would still love to have one day.

In the event, Wales turned to Bobby Gould as their new manager. By the time he arrived, Europe was already a dead issue. His brief was to use the first year of his reign to build up a team ready to challenge for a place in the 1998 World Cup finals in France. It has been a somewhat tempestuous first season in charge for him, with Mark Hughes, Neville Southall and me all being left out at one stage or another. I'll admit that I wasn't at all happy about being told that, along with Hughes, I would not be in the team to face Albania, and then about being pulled off before the end of our 3–0 defeat by Italy.

But those who suggested that I was growing tired of playing for Wales, that I was ready to call time on my international career, were a million miles away from the truth. I have spoken to Bobby Gould several times and assured him that I am determined to win my place back in the Welsh side. And to help them get to France, which has to be my very last chance of ever playing in the World Cup finals. Gould took his fair share of flak for those decisions, but I urge everybody to get behind him and give him a fair chance.

We have, as ever, a tough qualifying group against Holland, Belgium and Turkey, but at least we have begun in the right vein by trouncing the minnows of the group, San Marino, 5–0 away from home. Second place in the group could be enough to get us a place in the finals – and I do not believe that is beyond us. We have a decent blend of youth and experience in the squad. And in Ryan Giggs we have a player who I believe is destined to rank alongside the very best in the whole world. It's four years now since Ryan first appeared for Wales, when he was still a teenager, being nursed along very carefully at international level by Terry Yorath.

He had shown his outstanding talents from the start and, after his brilliant first season with Manchester United, had already been heralded as the new George Best. That was a very unfair comparison to make. They are different players, from different generations. Alex Ferguson, Giggs' manager at Old Trafford, was determined that his precious young charge would not suffer the same fate as Best, who quit football prematurely after his years of high living in the media goldfish bowl. Giggs has been kept well away from the public eye until recently, when he has been allowed to talk to pressmen. I believe that Ferguson has handled his development superbly. It was a racing certainty that Ryan would suffer a reaction after his initial explosion on the scene – and he did, having a fairly ordinary season when those same people who were likening him to Best were all too ready to dismiss him as a one-season wonder!

But he quickly overcame that little hiccup and has since become better and better every season. He was absolutely brilliant for United over the past season. As well as his tremendous attacking flair, he is now learning to work harder for the team, and you'll see him running back and tackling opponents. While his team-mate Eric Cantona is without doubt a superbly gifted player and deserves all the praise and honours heaped upon him, my own feeling is that Giggs was an even more vital ingredient in United's Double success.

I've watched him maturing off the pitch as well, when we've been together with Wales. He's become accepted as one of the senior pros in the squad now. You have to make yourself remember sometimes how young he still is. Ryan is not a brash, forceful type of person but he's not shy either. I went to watch him in one game at Cardiff Arms Park last season, when I was absent through injury. I sat with him afterwards, just talking over a couple of points with him. And we finished up chatting for a long time. I think he could see we were both on the same wavelength.

Over the years to come he'll go through the kind of situations that I experienced with Wales, when I was probably the best-known player in the team. In particular, when you travel abroad to a game the local media hound you, wanting television, radio and newspaper interviews, asking your views on every topic under the sun. He will have all that to contend with – and when you're young it's far from easy to handle it. He will make mistakes, and will make the wrong comment to the wrong reporter, just as I have on occasions. Gradually you learn which pressmen you can trust.

But Giggs has the easy-going style to make him a great ambassador for Wales off the pitch. And, on the pitch, those extraordinary talents will give the whole team a lift for the next decade. With a genius like Giggsy in the team, you've always got a chance.

Chapter 12

The Predatory Instinct

Over the last sixteen years one question has dominated all others when people have talked to me about football – what is the secret of scoring goals? I just have to shrug my shoulders. I can't answer them because the fact is I don't know myself.

If I had to put scoring goals down to any one thing, it would be to pure instinct. It's as if your mind is being taken over by some strange sixth sense. Things just seem to happen that are beyond my control. You're almost living in a vacuum in that split-second before you score. I see myself running past defenders into open space, I see the goalkeeper ahead of me, I see myself chipping the ball over him or rolling it past him. But exactly why I'm doing these things is something I do not know or even understand. I doubt if I ever will. That is why the ability of goal-scoring is something you could never pass on to others, no matter how brilliant a coach you might be. It's something you are born with – if you're lucky.

If you could bottle the recipe, you'd have enough money to buy

Wembley! But I believe that all the great strikers over the years will give you the same answer as me. I have chatted about football to wonderful players from the past, the likes of Jimmy Greaves, Denis Law and Roger Hunt. We talked about goalkeepers or defenders, but never about scoring goals. I never criticize other players for missing good chances, either – because I have missed enough in my time. I know exactly how difficult it is.

There is also no such thing as an easy goal, despite what some people – those who never been strikers – might say. If I score a goal from a couple of yards out, it's because I have used that sixth sense inside me to be in the right position. If a goalkeeper fumbles a ball and I nip in to score, it's only the reward for the hundreds of times I have followed up shots or crosses to be in that position. There's no luck involved – just perseverance.

It isn't all down to instinct, though. Inspiration has to be matched by dedication. If I was to hand out advice to any youngster wanting to be a top centre forward, the first thing would be to master the basic skills of the game – passing, trapping, shooting and the like. That comes down to sheer hard work, to spending hours and hours, week after week, month after month, learning to strike the ball correctly. Then you have to learn the value of timing – on and off the ball. How to time your runs, time your passes. Sharpness off the mark is another vital quality – those first couple of yards are so important, to give you a head-start on the defender marking you.

You also have to learn to become single-minded, almost to the point of obsession. If you miss a chance – as we all do – you must have the bottle to be able to shrug if off, keep your head up and search for the next one. If a youngster can master all those things – and if he possesses that goal-scorer's instinct – he will have the world at his feet. And he will join that exclusive club that has the greatest job in football, he will enjoy the most exhilarating emotions of his life – scoring goals. It's what every striker lives for – and I can tell them that it remains just as exciting and fulfilling, no matter how old you get. I still get the same thrill I always have.

The goal that has given me most pleasure in my whole career is the second one I scored against Everton in the 1986 FA Cup Final. I hit it so hard it took the goal netting out with it and smashed the camera of a photographer who was sitting near the goal! It was a vital goal too, because it put us 3–1 ahead and it meant we had beaten our big rivals – and won the Double. That was the most memorable afternoon of my whole time at Liverpool.

I can recall virtually every goal I ever scored, but there are a handful that stand out in my memory. The best hat-trick of my career, quality-wise, came against Aston Villa in 1984. I hit one volley, which screamed in and then chipped Nigel Spink, who was a big guy, from just a few yards out. And all that came on a Villa Park pitch that was frozen solid. The game only went ahead because it was live on television. Oddly enough, I used to rate Spink very highly, but I always seemed to do well against him. It was the same with Neville Southall – scoring four against him in the Mersey derby in 1982 will always be a great memory, to a large extent because he was such a great goalkeeper.

I think the first of my two goals in the second leg of the European Cup semi-final against Dynamo Bucharest over in Romania in 1984 was a special goal – Graeme Souness set it up and I whipped the ball past a defender who came lunging in at me, and then chipped their goalkeeper as he threw himself at me. It was my one-hundredth goal for Liverpool and it helped us to win 2–1 and get to the final – a lot of people had thought we would be put out after we could only beat them 1–0 at home. But I enjoyed that victory so much, because the Romanian team were like wild men that night and 70,000 of their fans gave us some right verbal stick as well. It was great to shut them up!

Three of the goals I scored for Wales stand out. I got the only goal of our shock-victory over Scotland at Hampden Park in the World Cup in 1985 – a left-foot volley from the edge of the penalty area, which left the likes of Kenny Dalglish and Alan Hansen speechless for years! Scoring the only goal again as we beat Italy in Brescia in 1988 was a sweet moment. It was my last game on Italian soil after my tough season with Juventus – and I was delighted to show those Italians who doubted me that I really could score goals.

'Then I got the winner in our 1–0 victory over West Germany in a European Championship game at Cardiff Arms Park in 1991, running on to a long ball through their defence, sending the goalkeeper the wrong way with a shrug of my shoulder, and then slotting it past him. It was the first time Wales had ever beaten the Germans.

They are all great moments, great memories. But really, if you ask any striker anywhere what was the greatest goal he ever scored, they'll all give you the same answer – the next one! You have to look forward all the time in this game. You can savour every goal, but they have to make you even hungrier for the next one. That is the only way to remain at the top level.

As well as giving me a fabulous life football has made me pretty comfortable financially. I live with Tracy and our young sons Jonathan and Daniel in a lovely, big home, set in four acres of garden and woodland in the picture-postcard village of Caldy in the Wirral, Merseyside's exclusive stockbroker belt. While football has dominated my life, I have also developed a passion for golf and horse-racing.

I've had a few bob on the horses ever since I was a kid – just like my dad I used to own a horse, called Coast Boy, but it was a disaster. It only ran twice – and came in last, and last but one! I had to get rid of it after that. It cost me six thousand pounds, and that was ten years ago. As far as I was concerned, it was money down the drain. But I guess it taught me a bit of a lesson. I've only had part-shares of a few horses since, as part of a syndicate that has also included my mate Jan Molby. Maybe I'll buy a horse of my own again one day – my dream would be to see it win a race on the flat at Chester. But I'll be a lot more careful next time!

Frankie Dettori, probably the greatest jockey riding right now, has become a friend of mine. He sent me his picture, which has pride of place at home. But I've been lucky enough to meet a whole lot of famous people over the years. Jimmy Tarbuck would come into the Liverpool dressing room before away games in London and keep us amused for ages with his gags. I had a drink with Rod Stewart once at the airport lounge in Anchorage, after our plane had been diverted there and Kenny Dalglish, an old pal of his, introduced us.

Cilla Black is another big Liverpool fan – I've met her several times. I remember George Michael calling me by my Christian name once and thinking it was amazing that he even knew it. But I suppose that fame, for what it's worth, is in the eye of the beholder. If ever I needed proof of that it came when I went to see Pavarotti at a concert in Cardiff a year or so back. He was absolutely wonderful, and I was only too pleased to be invited back after his performance to a reception organized for him.

I just stood at the back of the crowd milling around him as he sat down for his supper. Then he spotted me – and let out a yell! 'Ian Rush, come over here and have dinner with me!' he shouted, gesticulating to those seated near him to make a space for me. I sat down next to him and he talked about football – especially Juventus! – for half an hour or more.

But when he asked me to eat, I had to turn down his invitation. Whenever I am in Cardiff, I nearly always eat with Ken Gorman, a good friend of mine and the man who of course helped me to write this book. I had promised to meet him for dinner after the show and couldn't let him down.

Pavarotti, as well as being great fun to talk to, was awesome – it still makes me shiver just to listen to him sing. How can anything sound so beautiful? But he's not quite my most treasured memory. That has to be when I met the Queen to collect my MBE. I have told you about that day. All I will add is that, from being a somewhat lukewarm Royalist before I met her, I became as avid a believer in the Royal Family as anyone could be. She is a genuinely sweet woman, with one of the toughest jobs you could ever imagine. I hope she rules for a long, long time yet.

Looking at the long term future I hope to remain in football after my playing days are finally over. And I don't rule out the possibility of forming a syndicate to buy a football club. It would have to be the right kind of club, with genuine potential. It would be fascinating to be able to organize and run the club from the boardroom right through to the playing staff.

Chapter 13

Tributes

Ryan Giggs
'Ian Rush stands out as my sporting hero. It was an ambition fulfilled to play alongside him for Wales. As a schoolboy I wanted to be a striker, so I used to watch players in that position closely. The three I particularly admired were Gary Lineker, Mark Hughes and Ian Rush. But it was Rushy who stood out.

'When I was an apprentice at Manchester United, Alex Ferguson and Eric Harrison, the youth team coach, used to tell me to watch Liverpool matches and study Rushy's movement, tackling and work-rate. Everybody was well aware of his goal-scoring abilities, but he is such an example to young players, with so many other strengths to his game.'

Paul Byatt (Mike Dixon in Channel 4's Brookside)
'I was just sixteen years old when I started going to the Kop – and Rushy became my hero straight away. It broke my heart when he left us to go to Italy. When he came back to Anfield after just one year it was like Christmas. Now he's leaving us again, this time for good – and it just won't seem the same watching Liverpool any more.

'I'll still go to watch them whenever I can. And maybe Robbie Fowler will go on to become just as great a player and goal-scorer as Rushy one day. But it can never be quite the same. There was something about Ian that every Liverpool supporter identified with – maybe it was because he always seemed like such a normal guy, no big head or glamour about him once he had left the pitch.'

Mick McGiven (former Ipswich manager, after a Rush hat-trick against his team)
'Rush is just a class act. He will go down in history as one of the true legends of Liverpool – and rightly so. You just dare not give him an inch of space in that penalty area or you will be punished.'

Paul Walsh (former Liverpool striker)
'I joined Liverpool when I was twenty-one years old because I wanted to learn from the best – Ian Rush and Kenny Dalglish. As a young player you have to take in as much as you can by watching them do it. You might have your own little tricks and things, but you must incorporate what the likes of Rushy do into your own game to help yourself develop.'

Mark Lawrenson
'Show me any list of strikers and I'd have to put Ian Rush at number one. England might have had their Gary Lineker, but Rushy was always better than him. As well as being a fantastic goal-scorer, he always had so many more facets to his game. His work-rate has always been phenomenal.'

Dennis Waterman (star of television blockbusters Minder and The Sweeney)
'I always loved playing football and I've played in charity games whenever I can. It was always my ambition to line up in the same

forward line as Rushy – and it came true up in Geordieland back a few years, when Ian was playing in Italy. He was injured and unable to play for Juventus, so he came to this particular game officially just to kick off.

'But I met him on the night before. We had a good few drinks and he was such a smashing bloke I asked him to play alongside me, just for five minutes. I know it was a bit unfair on him – he might have aggravated that injury. But he started the game anyway – and he stayed on half an hour until he scored a goal! I'd always been a big fan of his, but that day he went right up to the sky in my estimation. I like to think I can call him a friend now.'

Robbie Fowler

'I used to hate Ian Rush when I was young, because I was a devout Evertonian in those days – and he seemed to score every time Liverpool played against us. It's strange to think he used to support Everton, too, when he was a kid. Since I've been at Anfield he has been brilliant to me, always giving me good advice and never showing any kind of envy at all.

'He would talk to be before every game, telling me the strengths and weaknesses of the defenders we would be facing. Then, out on the pitch, he would be telling me when and where to make my runs. I suppose it's inevitable that people will compare us, but Rushy's just in a different class from me. His finishing, passing, the way he holds the ball up...everything really.'

David Moores (Liverpool Chairman)

'We are frequently told that records are made to be broken, but I wonder if the extraordinary goal-scoring achievements of Ian Rush will ever be equalled. Not only that, Ian has remained unaffected by his success and a great ambassador for Liverpool.'

Jimmy Mullen (former Burnley manager)

'Ian Rush epitomizes the spirit of Liverpool in their successful years. For a striker, his work-rate is absolutely phenomenal and his finishing is awesome. He has to be among the greats. I say to any young striker that if they ever want to set their standards, then they should watch Ian Rush.'

Kevin Ratcliffe (former Wales captain)

'We used to be room-mates for Welsh games and he was the most untidy so-and-so you could ever come across! But his commitment and effort for Wales were totally one hundred per cent. And there was no edge to him, either. He might have been the biggest star name in the team, but he was always just one of the lads.

'Playing against him for Everton was a different matter, mind you. There was no quarter asked, or given, then. He used to be public enemy number one as far as I was concerned, because of all those goals he scored against us.'

Jurgen Klinsmann

'I admire Ian because he is not just a great scorer. He has a wonderful instinct inside the box, but it is as a team player that he excels. He opens up space for other players, fights hard and, for a forward, wins an amazing number of balls back.'

Emlyn Hughes (former Liverpool captain)

'In Anfield folklore, Rush belongs in the same class as Kenny Dalglish and Kevin Keegan. And as a hitman, I put Rushy up there with Jimmy Greaves and Roger Hunt as the greatest I have seen. We'll never see his like again, because players like him are a dying breed.'

Roger Hunt (Liverpool's former record goal-scorer)

'Ian Rush broke my records in probably the toughest era for forwards we've ever seen in the British game. That's why I admire him so much. I played at a time when defences were more open, teams played with wingers and, frankly, it was easier to score goals.

'After the 1966 World Cup, teams developed a greater emphasis on defence. But he stuck at it through those tough times when defenders were having it all their own way – and still kept scoring goals at a phenomenal rate. The top young strikers today have the benefit of starting out at a time when the rule changes are giving some of the advantage back to the forwards.

'That's going to be a big help to them. If Rushy had played in my time, or was just starting out now, he would probably get one hundred more goals than he has already.'

Ron Atkinson

'I'll tell you how good Ian Rush is – if Rushy had been playing for Manchester United during my five years there, instead of for Liverpool, we would have won three Doubles and a Treble. And I'm being deadly serious. Since he established himself in the Liverpool team he became as good a goal-scorer as I've ever seen. He's maybe the best of all time.

'And I include the likes of Jimmy Greaves and Denis Law in that list. Remember, Rushy has done the business in the modern game, when the defensive set-ups and sweeper systems are that much harder to dismantle. He's a killing machine in front of goal.'

Appendix

By Ken Gorman

Ian Rush scored 346 goals in 658 appearances for Liverpool, a phenomenal total unmatched by any other Premiership or First Division player in football's recent history. The goal ratio – more than one for every two games – is all the more remarkable when you consider that many of those appearances were as a substitute, when he did not play the full ninety minutes.

His goals tally is as follows: 229 in the League, forty-eight in the League Cup, thirty-nine in the FA Cup, twenty in European ties, three in the Charity Shield and seven in the Screensport Super Cup, an official competition organized for top English clubs during the ban from Europe. He also scored fourteen League goals and three FA Cup goals for Chester; eight League goals, five in the Italian Cup and one in Europe for Juventus; and twenty-eight goals for Wales.

He holds the all-time scoring records for both Liverpool and Wales, is the highest scorer in the history of the FA Cup and stands just one goal behind Geoff Hurst's record for League Cup goals. His five goals in three FA Cup Finals is another record, while his incredible haul of twenty-five goals against Everton represents the most ever notched up by one man in Merseyside derby games. The only record that he failed to capture at Liverpool was their all-time

League goals total, held by Roger Hunt with 245 – just sixteen more than Rush.

His roll of honour includes five League Championship medals, five League Cup victories, three FA Cup successes and one European Cup victory. He has also captained both Liverpool and Wales. Ian Rush has been fêted as one of the greatest goal-scorers of all time.

But the story is not over yet. His summer move to Leeds has given his career a new impetus, a chance to show that there are still challenges to be met, honours to be won, goals to be achieved. 'I am as excited right now as I have been for many years,' he says, words that will worry defenders around the world. The legend of Ian Rush is not finished yet.